FRUITFUL

Abiding in Christ as seen in John 15

LIFE

Text copyright © Tony Horsfall 2006
The author asserts the moral right
to be identified as the author of this work

Published by
The Bible Reading Fellowship
First Floor, Elsfield Hall
15–17 Elsfield Way, Oxford OX2 8FG
Website: www.brf.org.uk

ISBN 1 84101 335 8
ISBN-13 978 1 84101 335 0
First published 2006
10 9 8 7 6 5 4 3 2 1 0

Acknowledgments
Scripture quotations taken from the Holy Bible, New International Version, copyright
© 1973, 1978, 1984 by International Bible Society, are used by permission of
Hodder & Stoughton Limited. All rights reserved. 'NIV' is a registered trademark of
International Bible Society. UK trademark number 1448790.

Scripture quotations from THE MESSAGE. Copyright © by Eugene H. Petersen 1993,
1994, 1995. Used by permission of NavPress Publishing Group.

Extracts from the Authorized Version of the Bible (The King James Bible), the rights
in which are vested in the Crown, are reproduced by permission of the Crown's
patentee, Cambridge University Press.

A catalogue record for this book is available from the British Library

Printed in Singapore by Craft Print International Ltd

A
FRUITFUL
Abiding in Christ as seen in John 15
LIFE

TONY HORSFALL

Dedicated to my friends at Ashburnham Place in Sussex:
Andrew and his team of permanent staff and volunteers,
for making me so welcome and having faith in me;
and to all those who have attended my courses and retreats in
this beautiful place over the last few years, my thanks for
responding so well and taking me to your hearts.

Acknowledgments

My thanks to all those writers who, by their work, have inspired me to draw closer to God and learn how to abide more fully in Christ; and their publishers for permission to quote from their writings.

Special thanks to Barbara Parsons for the poems, prayers and meditations included in this book. May your gift find the recognition it deserves, and may you continue to bear your own unique kind of fruit.

CONTENTS

The harvest of the Vine: natural outcomes

The challenge of the Vine: learning the lessons

JOHN 15:1–17

I am the true vine, and my Father is the gardener. He cuts off every branch in me that bears no fruit, while every branch in me that does bear fruit he prunes so that it will be even more fruitful. You are already clean because of the word I have spoken to you. Remain in me, and I will remain in you. No branch can bear fruit by itself; it must remain in the vine. Neither can you bear fruit unless you remain in me.

I am the vine; you are the branches. If a man remains in me and I in him, he will bear much fruit; apart from me you can do nothing. If anyone does not remain in me, he is like a branch that is thrown away and withers; such branches are picked up, thrown into the fire and burned. If you remain in me and my words remain in you, ask whatever you wish, and it will be given you. This is to my Father's glory, that you bear much fruit, showing yourselves to be my disciples.

As the Father has loved me, so have I loved you. Now remain in my love. If you obey my commands, you will remain in my love, just as I have obeyed my Father's commands and remain in his love. I have told you this so that my joy may be in you and that your joy may be complete. My command is this: Love each other as I have loved you. Greater love has no one than this, that he lay down his life for his friends. You are my friends if you do what I command. I no longer call you servants, because a servant does not know his master's business. Instead, I have called you friends, for everything that I learned from my Father I have made known to you. You did not choose me, but I chose you and appointed you to go and bear fruit—fruit that will last. Then the Father will give you whatever you ask in my name. This is my command: Love each other.

FOREWORD

'Spirituality' is a slippery term today.

In Britain it covers everything from Zen to self-actualization. 'Spiritual' people can be cheating on their spouses, taxes and employers, and still consider themselves 'spiritual' because they 'meditate'.

In contrast, we need to rediscover the magnitude of what Jesus offers in making people whole again. That offer is nothing less than the very life of God in the individual's soul, making 'poor photocopies' of humanity into 'originals' again, into the very image of Christ. To that end, Tony Horsfall's latest book will help us on our way.

There is no better teacher than the Lord Jesus, so Tony acts as a competent guide to our Lord's marvellous and mysterious teaching on the spiritual life in John 15. He writes clearly and accessibly for all, and the book is full of practical wisdom and direction from a compassionate and competent pastor of souls. I found my mind informed, my heart warmed, and my will challenged again and again to yield unreservedly to the 'divine gardener' who tends our souls with a Father's love. I believe that will be your experience too.

As you will discover, the book can be used by both individuals and groups, hence the questions provided for further study. Groups are really important, since spirituality can become eccentric and cranky without others around us to keep our feet on the ground. Tony's chapter on 'Loving community' is vital: a local church fellowship is not supposed to be a penance we undergo for seeking to be 'spiritual'; it is a privilege!

The need of the hour is for Spirit-filled, Christ-centred, Father-glorifying, Bible-based, fruitful individuals and churches. This book can only help towards that goal.

Dr Steve Brady, Principal, Moorlands College

✜

INTRODUCTION

In this opening decade of the 21st century, the church in Britain and other parts of the Western world appears to be going through a major transition. Perhaps later generations will look back on this period and see more clearly exactly how significant a turning point the start of the new millennium proved to be for the church. For those of us living through this time of change, however, the shape of things to come is not yet clear. We know what isn't working, but we are less sure about what should take its place.

Changes in society, and the movement away from the certainties of modernity into the relativism of the postmodern era, inevitably affect the church. It is hard for us to hold to moral absolutes when, for most people, truth has become personal and individualized. Pastoral issues have become more complicated, while ethical situations that were once straightforward are now increasingly confusing and complex. It is not easy for the church to navigate through the moral maze of today.

Furthermore, we are living now in what is called a 'post-Christian' society, where the church and Christian teaching do not have the place of influence they used to have. Indeed, the church is increasingly marginalized and seen as irrelevant to life today. To reach a post-Christian generation, which sees Christianity as having failed, is much more difficult than winning pre-Christian generations, for whom the gospel message was splendidly new and relevant.

In addition, our society is now definitely multi-faith, with most of the world religions firmly established and religious tolerance the accepted norm. In a pluralistic world, Christianity is seen as only one of several possible options. No wonder, then, that the materialistic and pleasure-seeking pagans of our day give little thought to the church and what it offers.

Numerical decline has affected all the mainstream denominations, with a disturbing exodus of young people. It is common to speak of the 'greying' of the church. Of course there are exceptions to this trend, especially among some of the black churches and a few potential suburban mega-churches, but these are the exceptions. For most congregations and church leaders, this is a time of struggle. There is a lack of confidence in the gospel, a confusion about how we apply Christian standards in a world that has none, and a weariness from working hard for little result.

All is not lost, however, for God has not abandoned his church— and will not do so. Even where there is death, new life is already emerging. New ways of doing church are springing up as bold pioneers recognize that we must change or die. It is common to speak of the 'emerging' church. Searching questions are being asked. What does it mean to be church in the 21st century? How do we repackage the unchanging gospel for a postmodern generation? What forms and structures will be effective to reach post-Christian Britain?

If we are to win new people for Christ and arrest the numerical decline and drift from our churches, it is obvious that something radical needs to happen. We cannot bury our heads in the sand. Change must take place, and fundamental change too, which gets right to the heart of the matter. We must look at how we do church, and somehow get back to the essence of what church is really all about.

I believe we also need to take a step further back, and ask an even more fundamental question. It is this: how do we live the Christian life? It is one thing to change the external forms and structures of church, but unless we rediscover what it actually means to live the Christian life, I fear that in another ten years our new forms of church will prove just as inadequate as the old ones. The real question is, 'What does it mean to be a Christian?'

One of the most fundamental reasons why people leave church is because they have never understood how to live the Christian life. It seems too difficult, and it doesn't seem to work. Organized religion, with its structures and hierarchies, its buildings and its programmes, has somehow managed to strangle the life out of a living relationship with Jesus Christ. It has all become too complicated, and the simplicity of knowing Jesus has been lost. Burdened with rules and expectations, and weary from trying hard, we have nothing of vitality to offer to a lost world. If we are not thrilled with church, why should anyone else be? If we are not excited by our faith, how can we pass it on to others, especially in such a hostile and unsupportive environment?

The first believers also lived in a hostile world, but they had a contagious enthusiasm about their faith. 'We cannot but speak the things which we have seen and heard' was their testimony (Acts 4:20, KJV). They were not perfect, of course, and the New Testament epistles reflect many of the problems they encountered, but they did have life—and that is what we seem to be lacking.

This is why I believe we need to rediscover what it means to live the Christian life, and why, in this book, I want to examine again the teaching of Jesus in John 15. Here the Master is preparing his disciples for his departure, getting them ready for when they will face a hostile world on their own. He describes for them how they can be effective and fruitful in their witness and service. He tells them how to live the life he has planned for them. Just as his instructions revolutionized their lives, so a proper understanding of what he is saying can revolutionize our lives also.

The heart of his teaching is not difficult. Through the allegory of the vine and its branches, Jesus points his disciples to a life of union with himself. It is, in fact, impossible to live the Christian life apart from him. He is to be the source of our life, and just as a branch remains in the vine and receives its life from the vine, so we are to remain in him. This is no mystical, pietistic teaching, but something that lies at the heart of the gospel message. The only way we can live the Christian life is to allow Jesus to live his life in us and through us. If we can get back to this basic principle, we can discover again the excitement and joy of Christian living, which will not only rekindle our own enthusiasm but can make us effective once again in reaching others. It can put new wine into the new wineskins (Mark 2:22) that are so desperately needed at the present time.

It is my desire, through these pages, to point you back to the simplicity of a life lived in relationship with Jesus Christ. A life of intimacy, of abiding in him, is the source and spring of all other activity and endeavour. The branch bears fruit because it abides in the vine. It is the natural outcome, an inevitable process of nature. We need not fear that by emphasizing intimacy we will become ineffective. True intimacy will always move us into God-initiated activity, and that is what produces fruit that lasts. Frenzied activity alone will not make a difference to our world. It is God-directed work that will prove effective, and that comes as we learn to spend time with him, abiding in Christ.

We like rules:
You know where you are
With a good law.

We like to accuse:
To say: 'You stepped over
The drawn line.'

Relationship
Does not have rules—
Just intimacy:

Christ in me,
His life in mine.
Forget the rules,
Just live.
BARBARA PARSONS

THE LESSON OF THE VINE:
CHOSEN FOR A REASON

1

LIVING WITH A PURPOSE

You did not choose me, but I chose you and appointed you to go and bear fruit—fruit that will last (v. 16).

This is to my Father's glory, that you bear much fruit, showing yourselves to be my disciples (v. 8).

Rick Warren, pastor of Saddleback Church in California, has done more than anyone else in recent times to call believers to purposeful living. Through his books, *The Purpose Driven Church* and *The Purpose Driven Life*, he has reminded us that we are here on earth for a purpose, and that our lives only have meaning as we discover what that purpose is and begin to order our lives accordingly.[1]

Warren leaves us in no doubt about what he considers to be the purpose of life. It is to glorify God. We were made by God, but also for God, and life is about letting God use us for his purpose. Many things can motivate us in life, but according to Warren the greatest purpose of all is to live to bring glory to God. This is what we were made for, and it is only in fulfilling this fundamental reason for our existence that we find meaning and satisfaction. A purpose-driven life, therefore, is a life that is guided, controlled and directed by God's purposes.

This seems to be exactly what Jesus has in mind as he speaks with his disciples towards the end of his earthly ministry. He is preparing them for the work he has called them to do, and reminds them first of all that he was the one who chose them. As he began his ministry, he carefully chose a small group of men to be with him and to learn from him. These were people whom he hand-picked, and with whom he shared his life. He took the initiative by inviting them to become his disciples, calling them simply but radically to 'follow me' (see, for example, Mark 1:16–20).

To this invitation they had responded with enthusiasm, and they had spent almost three years with their master, listening to his teaching, watching him at work. They had seen his miracles and experienced his power at first hand. They had pondered his parables, and when they could not understand he had talked to them privately, explaining things more clearly. Sometimes he had rebuked them for their lack of faith, but gradually they had come to see that he really was the Son of God, and the impact of his message began to change their characters and transform their lives. Now he begins to unfold to them the purpose behind their apprenticeship: that they might go into the world and bear fruit for God.

Jesus had thought long and hard before he designated exactly who should be among his closest followers. Only after much prayer did he call to him the Twelve who would become the foundation of what he wanted to accomplish, and who, following his death, would be the basis on which the church would develop (see Mark 3:13–14). These are the ones he is now addressing, reminding them that he has chosen and prepared them for this very task, and that he is about to send them out to put into practice all that he has taught them. The whole thrust of his teaching here is to show them exactly how they will be able to make an impact in the world.

While these words were spoken and directed specifically to that original band of twelve, in a general sense they are spoken to any who consider themselves to be disciples of Jesus, for the pattern of discipleship now is exactly the same. The only reason that any of us comes to faith is that God breaks into our lives and, in his divine initiative, calls us to himself. We have also been chosen, and chosen for a reason—that our lives might glorify God.

The purpose too remains the same. We are sent into the world of the 21st century to make other disciples, to bear fruit for God in our own society and culture. He 'appoints' us (literally, 'assigns' or 'allocates' us) to specific tasks. The fact that he has called us is the guarantee that he will enable us to fulfil his purpose. If he has called us to bear fruit, then he will show us how to bear fruit in our lives. We have a destiny, a divinely constructed purpose, and one of the most exciting things in the world is to begin to discover, and to live in, that destiny.

Of course it is possible for us to live for some other purpose. Because life only makes sense when we have a purpose, people usually find something to live for and to build their lives around. The sad thing is that they often choose to live for a small purpose, rather than the grand purpose for which God made us in the first place. So it is that many people (and believers can get caught in this trap as well) tend to live for themselves, often with the pursuit of happiness and material gain as their chief goals in life. God may be a welcome addition to their striving for contentment, a useful ally in a hostile world, and a kind of insurance policy against unhappiness; but basically they are living for their own purpose rather than for God's.

It is only when we begin to see the shallowness and emptiness of living for ourselves that we can begin to step out into the much bigger purpose that God has for us, and discover the destiny for which we were made. It is an amazing thought that the God who knows me intimately actually shaped and formed me with his purpose in mind, and that my greatest fulfilment in life comes as I embrace his will. It is then that I find my own true happiness, which lies in serving God and bringing his life to other people. In other words, it is my destiny to bear fruit.

What exactly do we mean by 'fruit'? My definition of fruit is simple: it is *the outward expression of the life of God within*. It can take many forms, as we shall see in the next chapter, but essentially we bear fruit for God when we allow Christ to express his life through us. We bear fruit when we allow our faith not only to work in us, but also to have an impact on the people around us in our homes and families, in our work settings and social relationships, in our local communities and in society at large. Such fruit is the result of God working in us and through us. It is not something we produce by our own efforts or good intentions, but something that has its origin in God himself. This is why it is fruit that glorifies God, and also why it is fruit that lasts.

Some years ago, the church where I was pastor invited a team of young people from Sweden for a week of outreach. We reasoned that a team of blonde Scandinavians would have a big impact in our small mining town, and that this would present many good opportunities to share the gospel. They certainly had an impact, but not quite in the way we expected. Their evangelistic style was very aggressive, and as they went out into the town to witness they confronted people head-on with the claims of Christ. At the end of their time with us, they claimed to have led almost a hundred people to faith.

Sadly, we discovered as we followed up on the names and addresses they had given us that not one of these 'conversions' was genuine. Many had given false names and addresses. Some denied ever making such a decision; others said they were no longer interested. Not one person ever came to church as a result of that outreach. It had borne a kind of fruit, but not fruit that would last, largely I believe because it had been accomplished by human persuasion and not by the power of God.

Such a negative experience should not be allowed to dampen our enthusiasm or to lessen our expectation, however. It is God's intention that we bear much fruit, so we should expect a lot and not be satisfied with a little. A disciple is someone who takes the claims of Christ seriously and seeks to apply his teaching in their daily life. One of the ways we demonstrate the reality of our discipleship is by the fact that our lives do impact other people for good. If we are truly disciples of Christ, and if we truly abide in him, we shall indeed have the joy of seeing our lives make a difference.

When this happens, God is glorified, and that is the chief goal of any disciple. It glorifies God when ordinary believers allow God to take them in their weakness and inadequacy and work through them to the blessing of other people. 'We have this treasure in jars of clay,' says Paul, 'to show that this all-surpassing power is from

God and not from us' (2 Corinthians 4:7). The more we are aware of our inability to bear fruit by ourselves, the more we depend upon God, and the more it can be seen that any fruit comes from him, and not from us. The fact that God can take weak and sinful human beings and fulfil his purposes for the world through them is something that amazes both angels and demons, and brings glory to God. It is also wonderfully satisfying to be used by God to bless others, especially when we are aware of our own inadequacy.

Andrew Murray was a minister in South Africa over a century ago. He was a great devotional writer with a passion for those without Christ. In his little book on John 15 he makes an impassioned plea for his readers to grasp the fact that it is God's will that their lives should bear fruit, and much fruit at that. He urges them not to be the kind of disciples who are not interested in service, and whose lives produce little, but rather to be those who take the words 'much fruit' seriously and ask God that it may be so in their lives. 'The world is perishing, the church is failing, Christ's cause is suffering,' he says. 'Though you scarce see what it implies or how it is to come, say to Him that you are his branch to bear much fruit; that you are ready to be His disciple in His own meaning of the word.'[2]

We need this same passion in our hearts in our own day and generation. The need is just as great, probably even greater, for those who will take discipleship seriously and make themselves available for God to fulfil his purpose through their lives.

✤

Under a bed,
The child found a dainty comb:
Dull and dusty
Destined for the boot-sale.
She kept it
Because she liked it.

The expert,
Eyeglass in hand
Smiled with pleasure.
'This comb is old'
He said,
'And these pretty stones
Are diamonds.'

'It was made
For a royal queen
To be worn in her hair,
To be marvelled at
And envied.
Where did you say you found it?'

And you, child of God,
Were made for the King,
Chosen to bring Him glory,
For a royal destiny
And the highest calling,
Not to be lost
In the dust of small purposes.

BARBARA PARSONS

2

BEARING FRUIT FOR GOD

… that you bear much fruit (v. 8).

The branch of the vine exists for one thing only: to bear fruit. It has no other purpose, for the wood of the vine has no use of its own. At best it is used for making fires, never for making furniture or in building things or some other independent purpose. No, the vine branch is there solely to bear fruit.

We have already said that by 'fruit' we mean the outward expression of the life of God within, and it is important that we are clear about this definition. Much confusion (and sense of inadequacy) derives from the fact that many people have a limited, narrow view of what we mean by 'fruit'. For many, 'fruit' can be defined only in terms of people being converted. In this sense, we bear fruit by leading other people to faith in Christ. Given this narrow definition, many Christians think that they bear little fruit, and become discouraged. Leading others to faith is certainly one 'outward expression of the life of God within', but it is not the only one or, indeed, the main one.

As far as I can see from reading the scriptures, the main way in which the life of God expresses itself through us is in the formation of the fruit of the Spirit, described for us in Galatians 5:22–23. If the life of Jesus is at work within us, it will create within us the same outward expressions that characterized his earthly life: love, joy, peace, patience, kindness, goodness, faithfulness, gentleness and self-control. We can see each of these beautiful characteristics fully formed in the life of Jesus, and as we learn to abide in him they are naturally formed in us as well. It is worth taking time to savour each of the qualities listed here, for each is important and each has its unique and special value.

It is important to see that these Christian virtues are not external additions, like decorations tied on a Christmas tree. They are not developed by will-power or created by human effort, but by the life of Christ within us. Neither are they artificial look-alikes, as with some kinds of plastic fruit and flowers that can look so real. We are not imitating Christ, trying to be like him, copying his behaviour and doing our best to resemble him. Rather, we are expressing his life. The authentic fruit of the Spirit appears in our lives naturally as we allow his life to fill us and control us.

Take patience as an example. A recent news report spoke of the increase in anger at work. When people get stressed, they easily lose their patience and express their frustration in inappropriate ways. Life today, with all its pressures, means that there is more anger around. Road rage, for example, is increasingly common. How, then, can we become more patient? By trying harder? By learning the techniques of anger management? By biting our tongue? These may help to control our anger, but they do not actually make us more patient. The way to become more patient is to allow Jesus, the patient one, to live within us and express his patience through us. Because he is patient, and we share his life and his nature, we too can become patient. His patience can be reproduced within us. The more we receive his life into us, the more like him we become. This is exactly what it means to be a branch that abides in the vine.

Not only do we produce the fruit of the Spirit, but we express the life of Christ within us through acts of kindness and compassion—what the Bible calls 'good works'. Just as Christ was compassionate and merciful, healing the sick and caring for the poor, so we begin to share his heart for the needy and the hurting, and are moved to take compassionate action. Again, this is very different from some external forms of 'charity', done out of obligation or social conscience. It is actually Christ living his life through us. It is Jesus reaching out to others through us, using our hands to touch the brokenness in our world, continuing his ministry through our lives.

The apostle Paul speaks about this kind of fruit in his prayer for the Colossian believers: 'And we pray this in order that you may live a life worthy of the Lord and may please him in every way: bearing fruit in every good work, growing in the knowledge of God' (Colossians 1:10). Down the centuries, Christians have always been at the forefront of caring for others. We see examples in the New Testament and in the pages of church history. We think of Shaftesbury and Wilberforce, of Mother Teresa and Jackie Pullinger, and countless other lesser-known individuals. We have only to look around us now to see that where there is need in the world, Christian people are there, seeking to alleviate pain and suffering. Whether it be the fight against Aids, working with drug addicts, caring for the abused, feeding the starving, ministering to down-and-outs, meeting the needs of street children, or helping the homeless and the elderly, Christian compassion has moved people to get involved, on every continent of the world.

There are some who feel that an emphasis on intimacy with God detracts from involvement in the world and leads to a pietistic withdrawal. It is not so. If abiding in Christ brings us more fully into the stream of God's life, it will inevitably move us out into the world, for it results in an outward expression of the compassion of Jesus that grows within us. It is another way of bearing fruit for God and fulfilling the purpose for which we were made in the first place.

It should not surprise us that people who are expressing the life of Jesus by producing the fruit of the Spirit, and are demonstrating his compassion through their actions, have a certain 'attractiveness' about them. In a very natural way, and as much by who they are as by anything they say, they are able to point others to Jesus. Evangelism is one of the fruits of abiding in Christ, because Christ is the Saviour of the world. His concern for non-believers makes itself known through us, but always in ways that are appropriate and sensitive to where people are in terms of faith. It is never offensive, overly confrontational or argumentative. It is more about being led by the Spirit, recognizing when he is at work in someone's life, earning the right to speak, and responding to the opportunities for witness that he creates. This is the kind of evangelism that is fruitful, for it has its origin in God and is not simply the product of human zeal or enthusiasm.

The Bible tells us, 'The fruit of the righteous is a tree of life, and he who wins souls is wise' (Proverbs 11:30). People come to Christ as part of a process, often over a period of time. They move from knowing nothing about him to the place where they are ready to commit their lives to him, and there are many significant steps in between. Sometimes we have the joy of being there at the moment of conversion, when the final step is taken. At other times our witness may help someone move a step nearer to Christ. In both cases, we are bearing fruit. Fruitful evangelism is not about the number of 'scalps' we have taken. It is about being obedient to the leading of the Spirit, sharing from the life of Christ within us, and expecting that to make some kind of difference in someone's life. It is God who determines the outcome.

One final type of fruit needs to be mentioned. A natural outcome of the life of Christ within us is that we want to worship God. Just as Jesus lived to bring glory to his Father, delighting in pleasing him and doing his will, so there is created within us a joy in worshipping God. As the writer to the Hebrews says, 'Through Jesus, therefore, let us continually offer to God a sacrifice of praise—the fruit of lips that confess his name' (Hebrews 13:15).

It is fairly easy to worship God when life is going well. It is easy to praise him when things are working out as we want them to. It is altogether different to be able to give thanks and praise to God when we are struggling, facing difficulties, or feeling under attack. It is only as the life of Jesus wells up within us that we can praise God in all circumstances, and continue to worship him. This is when worship becomes a sacrifice, something that springs from the depths of our being, a trusting response of love to the God who is in control of our lives. There is nothing artificial or made-up about such worship. It is only possible for someone who is abiding in Christ and whose life is deeply connected to him. It is precious to God and glorifying to him, because it is really the expression of his own life within us.

We may not always be aware ourselves of the fruit being produced in our lives. Indeed, because it is produced by the life of Christ within us, it is largely unselfconscious and we hardly recognize it ourselves. Further, it may feel so natural to us that we would not label it as 'fruit', thinking that it is just normal when in fact it is the working of God within us.

Take my friend Julia, for example. She often feels that she bears no fruit for God, but anyone else looking at her can see that she is very fruitful, especially in her character. In fact, she is an inspiration to many, but she doesn't see herself that way.

Julia is disabled, lives with a lot of pain, and has been in and out of hospital most of her life, yet she never grumbles or complains. One day the wife of her home group leader was in hospital, and Julia decided to visit her. It meant a journey by rail to the city where the hospital was located, having made arrangements to be met at the station so that she could board the train with her wheelchair. When she arrived, it involved taking a taxi to the hospital, and then negotiating her way along endless corridors in a completely new environment until she found the ward—and all this again, in reverse, on the return journey.

'And was your friend glad to see you?' I asked Julia.

'Of course,' she said. 'She was delighted.'

'And don't you think you were bearing fruit when you made that visit?' I asked.

She looked puzzled for a moment, then slowly smiled. Almost reluctantly she conceded the point. 'Well, yes, I guess so.'

Julia couldn't see the fruit in her own life. What she did that day in visiting the hospital was the outward sign of the life of God within her. The compassion she felt for her friend, and her determination to get to the hospital, were the expression of the life of Jesus. She was simply bearing fruit out of her relationship with him. It was God at work in her life.

I think too of some of my friends called to bear witness for Christ in the least evangelized parts of the world. Responding to Christ's call, they have gone to live among unreached people groups in countries where other religions hold sway. There they faithfully live out the Christ-life before a watching (and largely unresponsive, sometimes hostile) world. Because their converts are few, does it mean that they are not bearing fruit? I don't think so. Their dedication to Christ, faithfulness in service and compassionate ministry are the fruit they bear, and in large measure. One day they hope to see a more tangible harvest, but for now the Lord of the harvest is delighted that they are willing to bury themselves in these remote places so that the ground can be tilled in preparation for what is yet to come forth.

The fruit of the Spirit, compassionate action, sensitive faith sharing and joyful worship—these are just some of the ways in which we can bear fruit for God. Anyone who chooses to abide in Christ as a branch abides in the vine can have the privilege and joy of seeing their life make a difference. As we give ourselves over to God's purpose, even our ordinary little lives can count for eternity.

If a man planted a tree
Watered it; cared for it.
And it grew leaves and branches
Yet it produced no fruit,

His neighbour would not say
'Shame on that branch; that leaf.'
But would shake his head, and sighing
Would blame the man himself.

Another tree: each branch
Fruit-bowed. Abundantly.
This time, the neighbours come
To praise both Man and tree!

BARBARA PARSONS

THE ALLEGORY OF THE VINE: LEARNING FROM NATURE

3

THE TRUE VINE

I am the true vine (v. 1).

I love to watch Jesus at work in the Gospel accounts of his ministry. He was a master storyteller, taking ordinary human situations and filling them with drama and interest, weaving into his narrative both humour and pathos, illustrating profound spiritual truth in very natural ways.

Stories like the prodigal son, the lost sheep, or the good Samaritan are typical examples. As a teacher, he is unsurpassed, using common, everyday objects and the incidents of normal daily life to create windows of revelation for his hearers into the deeper dimensions of life. Farmers, fishermen, housewives and shepherds all provide material for him, as do birds and flowers and trees. He presents simple, uncomplicated, ordinary truth for those who have eyes to see and ears to hear.

The allegory of John 15 is itself a masterclass in the art of teaching. Taking something as commonly seen as a vine, and drawing on the disciples' familiarity with the work of a vine dresser, Jesus unfolds in the simplest of terms one of the most profound mysteries anywhere in scripture: the believer's union with himself. Here is the art of communication at its best.

Perhaps the illustration had been suggested by a vine growing on the walls of the house where they were meeting for their last meal together, its branches hanging over the window and naturally catching their attention. Or maybe, as they left the house, walking towards the Mount of Olives, they had noticed the vines in the Kidron valley, and paused for an impromptu teaching session. It could even have been the golden vine upon the gates of the Temple that prompted the comparison. We cannot be sure exactly what gave rise to this memorable teaching. All we know is that as we read these verses we are privileged to eavesdrop on the Master's parting words to his disciples, as he prepares them for the work ahead.

Even the fishermen among the disciples would have recognized the wisdom contained in the picture of the vine. It was the dream of every Israelite to have his own house, with its own vine and fig tree (see 1 Kings 4:25). The countryside of Israel was littered with vineyards—row upon row of neatly tended trees, surrounded by stone walls and lovingly cared for by their owners. Grapes, raisins, wine: the fruit of the vine meant so much to everyone in Israel, and they were understandably proud of it.

This is a moment of self-disclosure by Jesus. He is saying something about himself, about his own identity. The words 'I am' occur frequently in John's Gospel, and each time they introduce a particular description of the Messiah, with a not-so-veiled allusion to his divinity.[3] Here he is saying that he is the true vine.

We might wonder why he chooses to liken himself to the vine rather than to some other tree—the olive, for example, which was just as common. Perhaps it is because the vine, with its tangle of branches, best represents what he wants to teach about union with himself and the importance of abiding. Maybe it's because the vine is kept for just one thing—its fruit—that it most suits his purpose, since it is the importance of fruit-bearing that he is communicating to his followers. There is truth in both answers, but almost certainly it is the connection between the vine and the nation of Israel that is the most striking aspect of this comparison.

Throughout the Old Testament, the vine is used as a symbol of Israel as God's people, and of his desire that they should bear fruit for his glory. Remembering the exodus event—how God had delivered them from Egypt and brought them into the promised land—the psalmist Asaph declares, 'You brought a vine out of Egypt; you drove out the nations and planted it. You cleared the ground for it, and it took root and filled the land' (Psalm 80:8–9).

Jeremiah adds his perspective too: 'I had planted you like a choice vine of sound and reliable stock' (Jeremiah 2:21). Hosea uses the same imagery: 'Israel was a spreading vine' (Hosea 10:1). Like an expert vine dresser, the Lord had taken care of his people and made every provision for their well-being and fruitfulness. His desire and expectation for harvest was clear: 'Sing about a fruitful vineyard: I, the Lord, watch over it; I water it continually. I guard it day and night so that no one may harm it' (Isaiah 27:2–3).

Yet the story of Israel in the Old Testament is a story of failure, for they never really fulfilled their purpose of making God's name known throughout the world. Favour and privilege led rather to complacency and waywardness. When God looked for a harvest, there was none. The divine disappointment can be felt in Isaiah's tragic love song:

> *I will sing for the one I love*
> *a song about his vineyard:*
> *My loved one had a vineyard*
> *on a fertile hillside.*
> *He dug it up and cleared it of stones*
> *and planted it with the choicest vines.*
> *He built a watchtower in it*
> *and cut out a winepress as well.*
> *Then he looked for a crop of good grapes,*
> *but it yielded only bad fruit.*
>
> ISAIAH 5:1–2

God was looking to find in the garden of his delight a sweet harvest of justice and righteousness, but instead it produced only the bitter grapes of bloodshed and distress.

When Jesus says that he is the *true* vine, he is saying two things. Firstly, he is the fulfilment of all the spiritual truth contained in the picture of the earthly vine. All the vines on earth are pictures and emblems of himself. He is the divine reality of which they are the created expression. Secondly, he is the fulfilment of all that God had hoped for in Israel. He too is a choice vine, for he is no less than God's own Son, and his nature is sinless and pure. He too had been brought out of Egypt (see Matthew 2:15), but whereas Israel through her disobedience had been fruitless, he through his obedience would prove fruitful.

What we have here is, in fact, a picture of the church. There is only one vine, and that is Jesus. The branches are joined to him, and what creates 'church' is the life that flows from him to the branches. It is an organic, spiritual, mystical union. This is a point that is often missed when we look at John 15, for it is usually interpreted from the perspective of the individual believer, when actually it is a corporate truth. Jesus is speaking about the new people of God, the church, which now exists to do the Father's will, and is the expression of his divine life flowing through its many members.

One of the lessons we can learn from this passage, therefore, is about the nature of the church, how God deals with his church, and the steps he takes to ensure that the church becomes fruitful. Any local congregation or Christian organization can look at itself in the light of this teaching. It is still equally legitimate to apply it to individual believers, however, and we will be doing this in subsequent chapters. Since it is true of all of us, it is true of each of us. The corporate and individual applications are both valid. What we note carefully is that it is addressed in the plural—to disciples, whether in the first or the 21st century.

I like the remark made by Matthew Henry in his commentary on this passage. He notes that 'the vine is a spreading plant, and Christ will be known as salvation to the ends of the earth'.[4] This is another reason why Jesus compared himself to the vine, and is in line with the prophetic hope of the Old Testament. Although Israel had generally failed to produce the fruit that God expected of them, there remained the conviction that his purposes would not ultimately fail. Isaiah expressed it like this: 'In days to come Jacob will take root, Israel will bud and blossom and fill all the world with fruit' (Isaiah 27:6).

All the purposes of God find their fulfilment in Christ. Everything is centred upon him and gathered together in him. As the true vine, he fulfils this expectation, and produces the fruit that brings glory to his Father. As we abide in him, we share in his fruitfulness and become part of the outworking of the eternal purposes of God. In Jesus the church takes root, will bud and blossom, and eventually its fruit will fill the whole earth (see Colossians 1:6). Where Israel failed, the church will succeed.

May we,
Your church,
Deep rooted,
Draw from your hidden spring.
May heaven's dew
Fall softly
And heaven's bounty bring.

So may
Your church
Bring healing
To this anguished world of tears.
And may Your church,
Christ breathing,
Buy back its wasted years.

BARBARA PARSONS

4

THE VINE DRESSER

My Father is the gardener (v. 1).

In the allegory that Jesus uses here, it is not just the vine and the branches that are important. There is a third aspect to the illustration. Equally as important as the relationship between the vine and the branches is the presence of the vine dresser. His role is crucial in the development of a healthy plant, and therefore in ensuring a good harvest.

The gardener is, of course, the person who owns the vineyard, and who is in charge of everything that happens there. He is the one who oversees the planting of the vines, who cares for their nurture and growth, and who ensures that they remain healthy and bear fruit. When Jesus says, 'My Father is the gardener', he is reminding us of his own subordination to the Father, and the fact that he lived his life under the Father's care and direction.

This is one of the great mysteries of the incarnation, for while Jesus was equal to God, for the purposes of our salvation he willingly subordinated himself to the Father, humbling himself and choosing to live in dependency and submission to him throughout his life on earth. We see this time and again in the Gospel accounts, especially that of John, who seems to have been most aware of the inner life of Jesus. Thus he records this statement of Jesus: 'The Son can do nothing by himself' (John 5:19).

Jesus lived in prayerful dependency upon his Father, constantly withdrawing to receive fresh supplies of strength, always listening to what the Father was saying, and watching to see what he was doing. 'I do nothing on my own,' he claimed, 'but speak just what the Father has taught me' (John 8:28). He lived to do the Father's will, gladly submitting himself to whatever the Father wanted, even to the extent of laying down his life (John 10:17–18; Mark 14:35–36). As he went to the cross, he confidently committed himself to the Father's care, knowing that he could trust absolutely in his loving purpose: 'Father, into your hands I commit my spirit' (Luke 23:46).

In this regard, Jesus' life is an example for us, for we too are called to submit our lives to the care of the divine gardener. Our heavenly Father is watching over our lives with the same care and authority that the vine dresser shows for the vine. As branches in the vine, we are called to yield ourselves to him and allow him to have his way in our lives. This we can do because he is also our Father, and all his purposes are for our good. We learn to live in dependency upon him, trusting in his wisdom and love in all the circumstances of our lives.

It is interesting to note the different ways in which the Father is described in various translations of the Bible. *The Message*, for instance, says, 'My Father is the Farmer'. A farmer is involved with plants on a commercial basis. For him it is a business, his livelihood, so he is looking for a harvest. He has invested time and money and resources into his fields, so he is rightly expecting an outcome. Likewise, God has invested in our lives and, quite justifiably, is looking for us to produce fruit.

Several translations (GNB and NIV) use the word 'gardener'. A gardener operates on a much smaller scale, cultivating his plants more intensely, and therefore developing a more intimate knowledge of them. He still looks for harvest, but has more time to be involved with each individual plant, valuing them and nurturing them. Here we are reminded of the individual way in which the Father deals with us. We are not lost in mass production. He has his eye on us, knows about us individually, and nurtures our growth accordingly.

A third term is 'husbandman' (KJV). Husbandry is the science and skill of looking after plants, and a husbandman therefore is one who has a keen understanding of the needs of plants and how to get the best out of them. He knows about soil and nutrients, the right conditions for the plants to flourish in, when to prune them and so on. His expert care guarantees healthy plants and a good harvest. How reassuring it is to know that the Father watches over us with the same expert attention, caring for our spiritual growth and formation with his infinite wisdom and using circumstances to create the right conditions for us to become fruitful.

Then, of course, there is the term that we have been using already, the 'vine dresser' (RSV). Here we have a person who is an expert in one particular kind of plant, the vine. He may not know much about other plants, but when it comes to vines he possesses an in-depth knowledge, possibly gathered from many years of experience in his own life and the lives of his predecessors. Who better to tend a vine than a vine dresser, one who really knows what he is doing? And who better to look after the spiritual well-being of his people than the God who made us, knows us individually and deals with us so skilfully? Truly we are in safe hands when we can say, 'My Father is the vine dresser'.

I have no first-hand knowledge of growing vines. The cold region of the north of England where I live is not noted for its vineyards! A friend once tried to grow grapes, but his vine yielded only ten fruits, all of them sour. Most of my information about vines has been gleaned from other writers, and the scriptures themselves. One of these writers is Robert Scott Stiner, and another is Wayne Jacobsen.[5] Both have significant insights into the qualities of a successful vine dresser.

Stiner recounts how he was in northern Italy, doing some writing, when he took a stroll in the area around his villa. As he walked and looked, he came across a vine dresser at work in the fields, a man called Aldo, who later became his friend and intro-duced him to the world of the vine dresser. Aldo was a hardworking man, always in the fields whatever the weather or time of year, diligently tending his beloved plants: 'Checking, always checking, always helping, always supporting. Doing what is best for those branches even if the branches don't feel it would be the best thing to do.'[6] The skill of a man like Aldo soon became apparent to Stiner, and watching him at work provided him with a new revelation of the Father's love.

Jacobsen, on the other hand, was raised on a 35-acre vineyard in California, and could literally say, 'This is my father's vineyard', for it had been in his family for several generations. He saw in his father many of the attributes of the vine dresser: the intimate knowledge of vines gained from years of experience, immense patience, lots of discipline and hard work, and a strong sense of purpose. 'In my father's vineyard,' he says, 'there was never any doubt who was in charge, who cared most deeply.'[7]

Years of watching his father at work in the vineyard gave Jacobsen a keen appreciation of the way in which God deals with us in our own lives. 'Since the vineyard is where I learned the most about God and about life, it is no wonder to me that when Jesus wanted to reveal the secrets of the kingdom to his followers he, too, chose a vineyard for his teaching tool.'[8]

The vine and the branches may have a wonderful union together, but without the skill and expertise of the vine dresser there is no guarantee that it will be a consistently fruitful union. We can almost feel the delight with which Jesus makes the affirmation 'and my Father is the gardener', for there is strength and security in the knowledge that the Father is there, so actively involved in bringing the vine to fruitfulness. It is not threatening to see the vine dresser standing by, looking on. His presence is reassuring for he is there to protect and tend, to train the vine and bring it to maturity and abundant fruitfulness. This is the ultimate goal of his tireless hard work, and the reason for his endless patience.

As we seek to live in relationship with Jesus, the true vine, we also become aware of the presence nearby of the divine gardener. He is there to bring us to maturity in Christ, and he will use whatever means necessary so that his good purpose for our lives can be realized. He does not bring us to the place of salvation and leave us there. No, he guides us on from that glad experience to the place where our lives become fruitful in his service. Patiently and tirelessly he trains us to become the people he wants us to be. He is always at work, and nothing happens to us that ultimately he cannot work into the shaping that is going on in our lives. His desire is that we too should be abundantly fruitful.

He is our Father, and we trust him. He is the gardener, and we submit to his will and his ways. Whether we think of this from the perspective of the church, or look at it on an individual basis, it remains wonderfully reassuring. Our Father is the gardener.

Like Father…

I look like my natural father
I speak with my sister's voice;
My son is a lot like me.
Same blood: same genes—
Same family.

I am a child of Almighty God.
To speak with my Father's voice;
To mirror the Saviour in me;
Like Father: like Son—
What destiny!

BARBARA PARSONS

5

THE BRANCHES

I am the vine; you are the branches (v. 5).

Few trees are as oddly shaped as the grapevine. The rough, flaky bark starts just above the ground and continues up the gnarled, twisted trunk to where it separates into craggy arms and on up to where the slender canes emerge. Twisting and turning, these new branches reach for the sky as the life of the vine pulsates within them in the first invigorating days of spring. Only the wise intervention of the vine dresser in tying them down and training them in the direction he wants them to grow prevents them from running wild. These are the branches that willingly express the life of the vine.

It is difficult when looking at a vine to see where the trunk ends and the branch begins. 'That is why Jesus couldn't have chosen a better illustration of the intimate bond he seeks with his followers,' says Jacobsen. 'He wants us to identify so closely with him that others cannot tell where he leaves off and where we begin.'[9]

The relationship between the vine and its branches does indeed beautifully illustrate what is sometimes called the 'mystical union' between Christ and the believer. It is a truth that is sometimes overlooked or undervalued, but it is a vital one, and the basis for all effective and fruitful living in spiritual terms. By 'mystical union' we are referring to the fact that, at conversion, God joins our life with the life of his Son in an invisible spiritual oneness whereby we are 'in Christ' and Christ is in us. This is not something that we do or could ever attain. It is done for us by a supernatural act of God. Neither is it something that we necessarily feel. It is something we accept as a fact, revealed to us by God in his word. This is why we speak of a 'mystical' union. It is brought about by the direct activity of God. It is unseen, spiritual, to be apprehended only by faith.

It is this truth that shapes the believer's identity. As far as God is concerned, I am 'in Christ', so completely one with him that God sees no distinction between his Son and me, the believer. From the moment of my conversion, God looks at me only as I am 'in Christ'. Just as the branch shares the life and character of the vine, so I begin to share in the nature and character of Christ. In him, I am counted as righteous and fully acceptable to God. This union I have with Christ becomes the basis of my confidence before God. Not only have my sins been forgiven, but I have been made righteous 'in him'.

The apostle Paul is often credited with teaching what it means to be 'in Christ', but in fact he was only enlarging on what was implicit in the illustration of the vine and the branches used by Jesus. Nevertheless, we are thankful for the revelation that Paul was given. 'It is because of him (God) that you are in Christ Jesus,' he writes, and, in explaining what this means, he adds, 'who has become for us wisdom from God—that is, our righteousness, holiness and redemption' (1Corinthians 1:30).

The other side of this wonderful truth of our union with Christ is that Christ is also now living in us. Not only is the branch in the vine, but the vine is in the branch, so that the vine's very life flows into the branch, sustaining it and causing it to bear fruit. This transfer of life from the vine to the branch takes place as the sap flows upwards from the roots deep within the soil. Through small capillary tubes, nutrients and water travel through the roots and trunk, and spread out through every branch until they reach every leaf and maturing bunch of grapes. This life-giving sap is what makes the branch into a fruitful bough.

The sap speaks to us, of course, of the life of Christ that we have within us. Again, this truth, implicit in what Jesus says, is made explicit by the teaching of Paul. We can live the Christian life only because Christ, who is our life, is within us (Colossians 3:3). It is him living his life in us and through us that makes it possible for us to live in a way that pleases God. Paul sums it up memorably: 'Christ in you, the hope of glory' (Colossians 1:27).

Here we have the heart of the gospel message: we are in Christ and Christ is in us. This is the 'mystical union' and the secret of our fruitfulness. It is a truth that we can fully understand only by revelation, when God opens our understanding to grasp the implications of being branches in the vine that is Christ. It is when we begin to live in the good of it that our lives really begin to make a difference.

There are two ways by which a branch becomes part of the vine. One is that it grows naturally out of the vine itself. The other is that it is grafted into the vine from another plant. This is, in fact, a common procedure, adopted by grape growers as it speeds the production of fruit. It can take anything from four to seven years for a vine to produce good-quality fruit, but by grafting new branches into an established vine, fruit of different types can be produced, and can also be grown more quickly. The process of grafting is described by Jacobsen:

Grafting is a nearly miraculous process in which one new plant is made out of two different ones. A branch is taken from one vine and inserted into a cut on another vine. The branch is bound to the new vine with an adhesive compound or tape. As the 'wound' heals, the two plants become one, the new branch drawing sap from the roots of the established vine.[10]

Perhaps this is a more accurate picture of our relationship with Christ, in that we are not there by right, but have been grafted in by grace. It is by God's initiative that we have been joined to his Son. This is something that Paul points out, and although he talks about being grafted into an olive tree, it is the same imagery and can be applied to the vine.

If some of the branches have been broken off, and you, though a wild olive shoot, have been grafted in among the others and now share in the

nourishing sap from the olive root, do not boast over those branches. If
you do, consider this: You do not support the root, but the root supports
you.
ROMANS 11:17–18

We have been made one with Christ as an act of God's grace and favour, not because we have a right to be there or because we somehow deserve it. We were 'wild'—uncultivated, uncared for, rebellious—but God in his mercy took us in and joined us to his Son, so that now we share in the life that he gives. This leaves us with no room for boasting, only with a sense of wonder and awe that this should have happened to us.

Notice what Paul also says here about the dependency of the branch on the root. It does not live by itself, and cannot support itself unaided. It is dependent entirely on the nourishing sap that comes to it from the root. This is what Paul means when he says, 'You do not support the root, but the root supports you.' We do well to remember this, for we cannot live the Christian life unaided. We were created for dependency, and the very weakness and frailty of the branch reflects this. Moment by moment and day by day it must receive life from its source, the root. So too must we, consciously and consistently, draw our life from Jesus the vine. He is the source of our life. Christ does not depend upon me to do his work. I depend upon him to do his work in me.

One further point can be made here, from something Paul says in the previous verse: 'If the root is holy, so are the branches' (Romans 11:16). In a very real sense, because we are joined to Christ in this mystical union, we share his life, his character, his very nature. What he is becomes transferred to us by the sharing of a common life. The reason we can produce the fruit of the Spirit is because his Spirit is within us, giving life to us. His Spirit has been joined with our spirit (1 Corinthians 6:17). We can become like Jesus because he is sharing his own pure nature with us. We can be holy because the one who is holy lives within us. Holiness is not so much about what we do or don't do; it is about the life that is within us.

The branch exists only for one purpose: to bear the fruit that is produced by the vine. As a branch by itself, it is weak and frail, fit for no other use than kindling for the fire. Only as it bears fruit does it find its purpose, and it does that by simply abiding in the vine. It doesn't have to produce the fruit, it simply bears the fruit that comes naturally through the life of the vine.

We need to remember that we are the branches, and that it is Jesus who is the vine. I am not the vine. I am only a branch. Yet as I live in union with Christ, and allow his life to flow into me and through me, I can have the privilege of bearing much fruit, and so bringing glory to the heavenly gardener.

The thing about true unity
Is the seamlessness of the join.

It is not an abutment;
An attachment;
A rigid locking together;
Detachable. Breakable.

Unity flows;
It melds;
The separate beings blend.
Inseparable.

It is oneness;
It is wholeness;
It is newness.

BARBARA PARSONS

QUESTIONS FOR REFLECTION

For individuals

1. What do you consider to be the main purpose of your life, and how does it relate to the purpose God has for you? How does it shape the way you live?
2. Remind yourself of the definition of 'fruit'. What 'fruit' is your life producing? What would help you to be even more fruitful?
3. What do you think is the main point of the allegory of the vine? How does it speak to you as an individual believer?
4. What is the role of the vine dresser? Why is it reassuring to you to know that your heavenly Father is the vine dresser?
5. How are you affected by the truth that you are in Christ, and Christ is in you? How will it help you to become more fruitful?

For groups

1. What is the pattern of discipleship that we see in these verses? What are some of the smaller purposes that people often choose rather than God's grand purpose for their lives?
2. What definition of 'fruit' is given? How does this help to remove confusion and a sense of inadequacy? What examples of fruit-bearing are given? What fruit do you see in each other?
3. Why does Jesus use the imagery of the vine, and why does he call himself the *true* vine? How is the vine a picture of the church?
4. What role does the vine dresser have in producing fruit? How does this speak to you as a group or church?
5. What do you understand by the term 'mystical union' and how is it an encouragement to those who wish to bear fruit for God? What are the spiritual lessons in the idea of being 'grafted in' to the vine? What encouragement is there in the fact that the branch has only to bear the fruit, not produce it?

THE TENDING OF THE VINE: KNOWING HOW GOD WORKS

6

SEASONS OF THE SOUL

There is currently a growing interest in spiritual direction. More and more people are discovering the value of having a mentor or 'soul friend' to guide them in their spiritual journey, and to help them discern the movements of God in their lives. It is indeed important that we learn to discern the 'seasons of the soul', and to understand what God is doing in our lives at any given period. The ability to listen to another with spiritual discernment is truly a wonderful gift to offer to someone else.

Although Jesus does not speak directly about the seasons and their effect on the work in the vineyard, it is implicit in the whole allegory, and I do not think we are going beyond scripture if we give our attention to the different phases in the work of the vine dresser. Each of the seasons brings its own particular characteristics, and the work of the vine dresser is to respond to the changing needs in the vineyard that come with each new season.

Spring brings rain and gentle sunshine, reawakening the process of growth that will come to maturity in the heat of summer. Autumn will be the time of harvest and ingathering, while winter provides a time of rest for the vine before another season of fruitfulness begins. The changing seasons determine the farmer's tasks and remind us that God works in our lives in different ways at different times. We also go through seasons. If we fail to understand that God works in seasons, we may well be confused by what is happening (or not happening) in our lives. As Jacobsen observes, 'The key to remaining in the vine is to look for the way God is working in our lives at any given moment.'[11]

SPRING

In the early days of spring the vineyard is at its best. The hard work of the vine dresser during winter has left it neat and tidy, and the vines, which have been pruned and cut back, are now bursting forth with fresh green leaves as the sap rises up from the trunk. Soon tiny clusters of white flowers can be seen, and as they pass away the first green fruit buds appear. This is a period of beginnings, of promise, of hope of a harvest to come. As the force of fruitfulness erupts from within the vine in an explosion of growth, new shoots and tentacles spread out in all directions.

This is the time for grafting in new shoots, while the sap is rising. It is also the moment for the first pruning, for too much growth will result in poor-quality fruit. Some of the suckers will need to be removed, some branches cut back, and even some grape buds removed so that the goodness of the vine is concentrated to produce the best-quality fruit. Above all, it is the phase when the vine dresser sets his pattern of care, for the young vine, in particular, must be trained for maximum productivity.

More than any other plant, if left alone the vine will grow wild. Not all growth is good, since too many leaves and shoots merely drain the vine of strength. In the early years, establishing a healthy pattern of growth is the most important thing, more important than producing fruit. The vine will need to be tied back and supported in its growth. Some branches will need to be redirected in their growth, perhaps tied to a stake or to another branch for support. Excess growth will need to be removed.

This season of rapid growth reminds us of the period of conversion and the early days of coming to faith, when everything is fresh and new. How important it is in the first formative months of faith (what we might call our 'first love') to establish healthy patterns for spiritual growth in our lives—prayer, fellowship, study of God's word, holy communion and so on (Acts 2:42). These simple spiritual disciplines provide the foundation for future spiritual growth and cannot be ignored. We should also recognize it as the period when God does the work of training us: bringing our will in line with his will, and ordering our priorities so that he has first place in our affections (Matthew 6:33). For many new disciples, the question of the lordship of Christ quickly emerges, and there is often a particular issue on which we need to surrender our will to his, if we are to continue to grow and become fruitful.

SUMMER

The hot months of summer are both a blessing and a curse for the vine. While it needs sunshine to bring the grapes to maturity, too much heat is very stressful for the vine, and can damage the development of the fruit. In a long, hot summer, there is also the danger of drought. Some farmers are careful to irrigate their plants, some even watering the most vulnerable plants by hand.

This is also a period when the vine comes under attack, and when the vine dresser must be most vigilant. Worms and parasites can attack the roots of the vine, and weeds, if left unchecked, can strangle the young plant. A host of insects and mites can attack the leaves. Caterpillars, for instance, can strip the leaves bare. Fruit-flies, worms and birds can devour the fruit, while diseases like mildew can assault the young grapes.

No wonder this period—between the promise of harvest and the actual gathering in of ripened fruit—is the most testing time in the vineyard. It reminds us that growth in the Christian life occurs often through times of testing and difficulty. As Jesus warned us in the parable of the sower, when the sun is hot (in the form of persecution or trouble), some plants wither because they have no root (Mark 4:5-6, 17).

At the same time, trouble has an amazing way of strengthening faith, and God sometimes allows us to walk a difficult path in order that our faith may be deepened. Robert Stiner discovered from his friend Aldo, the Italian vine dresser, that it may actually be to the vine's advantage to experience drought. In its struggle to live, the vine has to look much harder for moisture in the soil, and so sends its roots deeper and deeper into the ground. This results in a stronger and healthier plant. As Aldo expressed it, 'In order to make the best wine, the vine has to suffer.'[12]

It is not popular to speak of suffering these days, but the church has always grown best in a climate of persecution, and the suffering church has often produced the most mature believers and seen the most rapid numerical growth. We can expect to have seasons when 'the heat is on' for us as well. Trials cause us to depend more fully on Jesus, and it is suffering that produces character in us (Romans 5:3–4).

AUTUMN

Eventually the time for harvest draws near, and an air of excitement fills the vineyard as preparations are made to bring in the harvest. The vine dresser walks among the vines one last time, tidying and cleaning before the harvesters gather the grapes. The fruit itself is now coming to maturity, becoming softer and sweeter in the final days before harvest. There is no scene more beautiful to the vine dresser than to look around and see his vines laden with bunches of succulent grapes, all coming to perfection at just the right time. This is what he has worked for, the moment when his hard work and toil seem worthwhile.

Maturity is, of course, what the divine gardener is seeking to bring about in our own lives. It is that state of being 'fully developed', which Paul aimed to see in his converts. 'We proclaim him (Jesus), admonishing and teaching everyone with all wisdom, so that we may present everyone perfect (mature) in Christ' (Colossians 1:28). His goal was to see the life of Christ formed within them, and although it proved to be a difficult goal to reach, he never tired of working towards this divine objective (Galatians 4:19). While there is always room for us to grow and develop further, we should not forget that it is possible to become mature as believers and that this should be our objective as well. The passing of time should see a growing Christ-likeness in our character and an increasing stability in our walk with God.

Harvest is naturally a time of celebration. When the grapes have been safely gathered and stored, it is time to party, to relax and enjoy the satisfaction of a job well done. The fruit that is harvested is a reflection of all that has happened in the vineyard during the past year. If it was a good year, and the vines were well cared for, the harvest will be abundant. If the vineyard was neglected, the harvest will be small and the fruit of low quality.

We should not be afraid to ask ourselves the question, 'What is the fruit of my life?' This is not meant to condemn us, but to give us cause for rejoicing over what is already there, and to move us on to greater things, to desire even more fruit to be formed in our lives. We should never sit back in complacency and be content with the yield we have already produced. There is more that God wants to do in our lives, and we gladden his heart by sharing his desire for a more abundant harvest.

WINTER

Eventually the vines will shed their leaves, and the coldness of winter descends upon the vineyard. It may seem empty and barren now after the busyness of harvest, but there is still work to be done. The vine dresser is out there, mending fences, tying up branches, re-staking plants. Most importantly of all, he is busy pruning, getting the vines ready for another year of harvest. Excess growth must be cut off and the vines themselves tidied up so that they are ready once more for the growth that will come with spring.

Winter especially provides a time of rest in the vineyard, and it is important that the vines can lie dormant for a period. In fact, what is happening is that they are storing up nourishment for another season of fruitfulness, and this time of replenishment is important to the plant's well-being.

Seasons of inactivity, the winter months of the soul, can be confusing to us unless we realize that rest is as important as activity. Times of rich fruit-bearing can give way to periods of apparent barrenness, and unless we are aware that this is how God sometimes works, we may think he has abandoned us or that we are doing something wrong. This is not the case, however. We need times when we can draw near to God and be renewed spiritually. It is vital that, in the long haul of ministry, we have seasons when our aim is simply to have time with God and to be nourished in our own souls. Only as we take in can we give out. This is at the heart of abiding, for it requires us to spend leisurely time just being with Jesus.

Jacobsen reminds us that there are two ways in which God may bring us to winter. One is circumstantial, when the external activities of Christian ministry become less effective. The other is by calling, when God directs us to slow down and spend more time with him. This is the opportunity for retreat, to receive spiritual nourishment for ourselves and to be built up in our own faith. 'Spiritual winter,' he says, 'provides the Father opportunity to do an even deeper work in your life.'[13]

The cycle of care in the vineyard shows us that farming is often a matter of doing the same tasks year after year, repeating them time and again to ensure that the vineyard enjoys succeeding years of fruitfulness. It is not about producing a harvest once, but of repeating it year on year. As the relationship between the vine dresser, the vine and the branches develops, the branches become stronger and more stable and produce better fruit. God's work in our lives is an ongoing work, and the passage of time will see a growing spiritual maturity in our lives as we respond to his working within us.

The changing seasons also remind us that there is a rhythm to life, and that if we are wise we will learn to work with that rhythm and not against it. There are periods of busyness and activity, and times when it is right to rest and reflect. There are occasions of growth and expansion, and moments when we are cut back and restricted. There are phases of fruit-bearing and success, and passages of quiet when not much appears to be happening. It is all part of the maker's design, and the divine gardener is watching over us through it all.

✤

For my soul there is a season:
A time for renewal.
For passion;
For quick and sudden growth;
For budding and blossoming.
Then God must tame my wildness,
Lest strength be expended
With the passing of spring.

For my soul there is a season:
A time of fullness;
Of beauty;
Establishing and affirming;
The promise of all good things.
But of danger too, from the enemy's attack
To spoil and destroy
All that summer brings.

For my soul there is a season:
A time for fruitfulness;
Full bodied;
Ripening and bountiful;
Harvesting and rejoicing.
When hope becomes experience.
God's blessing is poured out
And the rich fruits of autumn
Are gathered in.

For my soul there is a season:
A time of bleak darkness:
Cold winter.
When life fills with sadness
And all hope lies dying.
But do not fear
The silence of winter.
For it does not speak of death,
Only of waiting.

BARBARA PARSONS

7

CLEANSING

He cuts off every branch in me that bears no fruit, while every branch that does bear fruit he prunes so that it will be even more fruitful. You are already clean because of the word I have spoken to you (vv. 2–3).

There is a ruthless determination about the vine dresser. He has one purpose in mind, and that is to produce a bumper crop. Everything he does is pointed in that direction, and all his tending of the vine is with this goal in mind: that the vine will be abundantly fruitful.

Pruning is the most important aspect of his care of the vine. Nothing is as essential as this to the fruitfulness of the vine, but it is an activity that requires skill, expertise and experience. To prune too much, or at the wrong time, will damage the vine and spoil the crop. Only an experienced vine dresser knows when and how to prune.

We see from what Jesus says here that there are two reasons for this pruning. The first is to 'clean up' the vine and remove whatever is detrimental to fruitfulness; the second is to cut off excess growth so that the vine can be even more fruitful. One is essentially a negative process, the other a positive one. In this chapter we will consider why and how the vine dresser cleans up the vine, and relate this to the cleansing work of God in our own lives.

It is interesting that the Greek word translated 'to prune' (*kathairo*) can also mean 'to purge' or 'to cleanse'. Cleaning the vine is an activity of spring, when there is much growth, a lot of which is wild and would drain the vine of life if left unchecked. Then, during the summer, the vine dresser is continually looking to remove that which is diseased or damaged, as this can affect the whole vine, and even the vineyard. This is also an activity of the autumn months, just before the harvest. Sometimes he will take off any big leaves that might be shading the grapes, so that they can dry in the sun, thus protecting them from the mildew that is spread through dampness. This thinning out also makes it easier for the harvesters to see the fruit, and makes sure that none of his precious crop is left to rot on the vine.

Jesus draws out a simple lesson from this cleansing of the vine. 'You are already clean,' he says, 'because of the word I have spoken to you.' Since the time when he first called them to himself, he had been teaching and training them. They had listened to his words in public and private, and that word had made its mark on them, cleansing their hearts and preparing them for future service. Their behaviour had been challenged, their ideas changed, and their understanding increased as he opened their minds to the truth of the gospel he had come to proclaim. He had exposed their sinfulness, but also shown them the way of forgiveness. His symbolic washing of their feet just a little earlier (John 13:1–11) was a reminder of the need for cleansing.

The same process of cleansing takes place in the life of everyone who wants to be a disciple of Jesus. The one thing that can prevent spiritual fruitfulness is the disease that the Bible calls 'sin', and the divine gardener is always active in our lives to remove its unhelpful influence. The way he does this is by speaking his word into our hearts. He takes the truth of scripture and, by the Holy Spirit, applies it personally to our need and condition.

It is the word of God that first convicts us of our sin. Although uncomfortable, the feeling of conviction is a healthy one, for it shows that we are responsive to God. It is in the Bible that we learn what is right and what is wrong, what pleases God and what doesn't. Having an objective standard to go by means that we can adjust our lives accordingly and are not left adrift in a sea of moral relativism or subjective values. This adjustment is what we mean by repentance, and we can expect the divine gardener to do some 'tidying up' in our lives, especially in the early days of following Jesus.

The process does not end there, however, for with conviction comes the message of forgiveness and the wonderful good news that when we confess our sins, God is faithful and just to forgive us, and to cleanse us from all unrighteousness (1 John 1:9). Again, through the objective word of God we learn that when we repent, God not only forgives our sins but removes them from us and remembers them no more (Psalm 103:11–12; Jeremiah 31:34). This means we have the assurance that our past has been dealt with, and we can now enjoy the benefits of a clear conscience. This confidence becomes the basis for a joyful, effective Christian life.

Next, as we expose ourselves increasingly to God's word, it begins to renew our minds, washing away our old sin-dominated thoughts and replacing them with a brand new perspective on life, so that our minds focus on what is good. A renewed mind is a clean mind, and again this is a prerequisite of holiness and spiritual fruitfulness.

At some point in this cleansing process, another truth is revealed to us—that our old sin-loving nature has been transformed, and we have been given a brand new nature that loves to please God (2 Corinthians 5:17). The truth of our new identity in Christ is foundational to the kind of fruitfulness that God wants to produce in us, especially the fruit of holy living. Once we realize that we have a new nature, we can begin to act accordingly. We are no longer under the power of sin, but with the daily help of the Holy Spirit we can live 'clean' lives consistently.

Of course, I am not saying here that we reach a stage of sinless perfection. There is still a struggle against sin, because we still have to contend with what the Bible calls 'the flesh' (the principle of indwelling sin), and sometimes we fall; but as we live in conscious dependency on God we can know an increasing victory over sin and temptation. There often comes a crisis moment where we make a radical decision to love God rather than to love sin. It becomes a turning point in our lives, because from that moment onwards we are pointing in the right direction, and become committed to living out of our new identity, not our old. Our hearts have been cleansed and sin is no longer our master. The power of evil has been dethroned, and Christ reigns instead. This sets the scene for us to be used by God and for our lives to bring forth abundant fruitfulness.

So far we have assumed that we are cooperating with the activity of God in our lives, but we all know that sometimes we do not respond to him as we should. What happens then? If we fail to listen to God's word and heed his spoken admonitions, then we come under what the Bible terms the 'discipline' of God. This may seem a surprising expression, but because we are his children, and because he desires our holiness, he will discipline us in love so that we learn to walk in his ways. The following scriptures make this very clear. 'Know then in your heart that as a man disciplines his son, so the Lord your God disciplines you' (Deuteronomy 8:5). 'Do not despise the Lord's discipline and do not resent his rebuke, because the Lord disciplines those he loves, as a father the son he delights in' (Proverbs 3:11–12). 'Endure hardship as discipline; God is treating you as sons. For what son is not disciplined by his father? If you are not disciplined (and everyone undergoes discipline), then you are illegitimate children and not true sons' (Hebrews 12:7–8).

These verses are worth pondering over and meditating upon. They show that God may allow hardship (in the form of various difficulties) to come into our lives in order to wake us up to the need to deal with our sin. He does this not in anger, but in love. It is the proof not that he rejects us but that he accepts us and is training us. And while it may be painful, it is for our good. If we respond and turn away from sin, we will share his holiness and joyfully bear the kind of fruit that is describes as 'a harvest of righteousness' (Hebrews 12:11).

Again, we are making the assumption that we are responsive to the discipline of God that comes to us through the hardships of life, but we must ask the question, 'What if we don't respond at this point?' If we persist in rebellion against God, and choose to hold on to our sin in spite of God's discipline, then it seems that we enter an even more serious level of cleansing. It is perhaps alluded to in the words of Jesus when he says, 'He cuts off every branch in me that does not bear fruit.'

Some commentators think that this refers to Judas, who was to betray Jesus. It may well be a specific reference to him, or it may be a general principle reflecting the loving determination of the vine dresser to have an abundant harvest. God will do what is necessary to make this happen, which includes removing branches that are diseased, damaged or dead. We must remember that God is 'not weak in dealing with us', and that it is 'a dreadful thing to fall into the hands of the living God' (2 Corinthians 13:3; Hebrews 10:31). There is a healthy fear of the Lord that prevents us from making light of sin and treating God's dealings with us contemptuously. It may not be popular or fashionable to think of this nowadays, but it remains true that the fear of the Lord is the beginning of wisdom (Proverbs 1:7).

There were some in the church at Corinth who persistently rejected God's voice and continued in their rebellious ways. Despite his patient pleadings with them, they continued to sin outrageously and without conscience, so God dealt with them for the sake of the whole body. Their failure to judge themselves meant that God had to step in, and, as we read in Paul's subsequent letter, many had become weak or sick, and some had even died (1 Corinthians 11:29–32). God had 'cut them off'.

We are not talking here about people losing their salvation. The whole tenor of scripture, I believe, is that once we are saved, we cannot lose that salvation. It is an act of God that even human sinfulness cannot undo. If we have been born again, we cannot be un-born again. We dare not be complacent, however, and think that we can live as we please. The words of Jesus here are a severe warning to us that we cannot be casual with sin or think that we can make a fool of God. Sooner or later he will act to protect his harvest.

Let me stress that what we are talking about here is the extreme of discipline, which happens only in occasional circumstances. It is not the norm. Most of us have the good sense to respond to God when he first speaks to us through his word. Occasionally we need a little stronger discipline, which—let us hope—we heed quickly and readily. Only in a very few cases does God have to take it as far as he did in Corinth. And always we remember that God's discipline is redemptive—not to punish us, but to win us back and put us on the right path again. It is always loving, merciful, purposeful and controlled.

We must not confuse this discipline either with the hardship that comes to us in the form of trials that are common to everyone. Discipline is because of sin, and if we are being disciplined by God he makes us aware of that sin. We know in our hearts what the sin is, and that we should be doing something about it. If we are not conscious of any specific sin, then we can assume the difficulties we face are part and parcel of life and are not to do with discipline. They are there to develop our faith and trust in God.

Those who deal with the sin in their lives, and cooperate with the working of God, are those who bear much fruit. The divine gardener is constantly watching over us with loving attentiveness, but he does require our responsiveness and willingness to work together with him. Unlike the branches on the vine, we are not passive. We can choose either to cooperate with God or to resist what he is doing in our lives.

✢

The child did wrong:
His father punished him.
There were tears
And anger,
But in later years
With children of his own,
He understood:
His father's training
Flowed from
His father's love.

A child did wrong:
His misdemeanour ignored.
No tears
No cries of 'It's unfair'.
But in later years
His life wild,
Unfruitful,
He understood:
His father's tolerance
Stemmed from
His father's indifference.

BARBARA PARSONS

8

PRUNING

Every branch that does bear fruit he prunes so that it will be even more fruitful (v. 2).

If cleansing enables branches that are bearing no fruit to produce some fruit, then pruning is the process by which branches that are already producing fruit are enabled to produce even more fruit. Thus pruning is the single most important activity of the vine dresser. It takes place continually, but mostly in the winter months after the harvest, and it is the way in which the vine is prepared for even more fruitfulness in the growing season to come.

Pruning has been described as 'organized destruction' and 'surgery of the highest order',[14] for when the vine dresser takes the pruning knife in his hand he is determined to cut away anything that will prevent the vine's increasing fruitfulness. Vines by nature grow quickly and erratically, and this wild growth must be dealt with, otherwise the sap will be used to produce leaves and branches rather than fruit. Fruitful branches, too, are pruned and some grapes removed, so that the nutrients are directed to the bunches that remain, making them larger and healthier. Even the branch itself is cut back, right to the vine. This causes it to grow in diameter later on, becoming thicker and stronger so that it can support more fruit in the coming season. Often, as few as only five branches will be left on the vine.

Spiritual pruning is the process by which God ensures that our lives not only bear fruit, but continue to bear fruit, and of increasing quality. Anyone who wants their life to glorify God will experience this work in their life as God cuts away from them anything that would hinder their productivity. It is often a painful process, and sometimes bewildering. We wonder, 'Why is this happening to me?' and often ask ourselves, 'How long will it continue?'

The sharp pruning knife that the divine gardener uses is once again the word of God, spoken directly into our hearts. It can come in a variety of ways—a scripture that we read, a sermon that we hear, the wise counsel of a friend, the quiet voice of the Spirit within, a word of prophecy, a parable of nature—countless ways by which God speaks to us and shows us what is hindering our growth, inviting us to let it go so that our lives can be more effective. We are not thinking here so much of sinful things as of things that are legitimate but unhelpful. In pruning us, God is dealing more with our self-life than anything else.

In my experience, pruning often centres around some key areas: who is in control of my life, how I use my time, what claims my affection, and the sources of my significance. Time and again I am brought back to the principle that God must be first in my life if I am to bear fruit for his glory. Through the combination of the convicting word in my heart and the trials of life, I am forced to reevaluate my life in order to bring myself more in line with God's will for me.

Selwyn Hughes says, 'The pruning process—cutting away the things that hinder or prevent our growth—provides for a continuous conversion in which we are converted from the irrelevant to the relevant, and from being just busy to being fruitful.'[15] There is no greater danger to spiritual fruitfulness than religious activism. If we are busy, we tend to assume that we are fruitful, but this is often far from being the case. Sometimes we are doing the wrong things altogether—things that we feel are right but have not been ordained by God. Sometimes we are doing too many things, all well-intentioned and good in themselves, but which leave our lives fragmented and distracted, lacking any overall sense of purpose or direction. We become like a wild grape vine, all leaves and branches, but precious little fruit.

Rather than living at sixes and sevens, God invites us to discover the power of a focused life, and to trim our activities down to those that he has given us to do. These are the ones that prove to be fruitful, and we find that we can do more by doing less. When God convicts us of being overly busy, we must respond and ruthlessly eliminate from our lives whatever is ineffective and not bearing fruit. It may require learning to say 'No' to people, establishing some boundaries, taking control of our diary. It could mean stepping down from certain committees, refusing that exciting invitation or opportunity, not responding to yet another 'need' that we see around us. In order to say 'Yes' to God we may have to say 'No' to some worthwhile activities. Calling us to reprioritize our time is one of the ways in which God prunes us.

Bruce Wilkinson, in *Secrets of the Vine*, makes a distinction between the pruning that takes place in the early years of our relationship with God, and that which happens when we have become seasoned followers. 'While early pruning is mostly about your outward activities and priorities, mature pruning is about your personal identity.'[16] I can see the truth in his remark, and it probably reflects my own experience, although any of these matters can be an issue for us at any time in our Christian lives.

Certainly I can remember the struggle, as a young Christian, to allow Jesus to be Lord of my life. So much seemed to get in the way of a whole-hearted discipleship. Sport was one thing, for I loved to play football and to watch it as well. It was painful, but necessary, that I surrender my love of sport to God so that he truly had first place in my life. Then he could give it back for me to enjoy in an altogether different way. There was a relationship, too, that threatened to shipwreck my walk with God. That also had to be given over to God, for it was a hindrance to my spiritual growth. These early moments of 'surrender' were the platform on which future ministry was built; without establishing Jesus as Lord of my life I could never have gone on to effective service.

Nor has the need for surrender disappeared. Even now, situations arise which reveal that Jesus does not have control over every area of my life. Just a few years ago I began to realize that God was preparing me to move on from my job of leading a missions training programme. While I was on retreat to pray over the matter, God spoke to me very clearly about stepping out in faith and developing a new ministry, one that would have its focus in South East Asia. The realization of what God was asking hit me very forcibly. The thought of relocating and leaving my grown-up children behind, and letting go of my lovely home, seemed too much to bear. It was another moment of surrender, of being pruned back in order to bear more fruit later on.

The decision I made that day has led me into a new phase of ministry altogether, and I have grown and borne fruit in ways I never expected. God opened up a new door of opportunity for me in Singapore, and although it has not yet been necessary to relocate, the surrender I made then was the basis for another season of fruitfulness. Letting go of what is precious to us is very much the human side of divine pruning.

One of the keys to a maturing discipleship is that we find our identity increasingly in who we are in Christ, and less and less in our own achievements or success. This becomes a testing ground for many of us, because it is so easy to derive our sense of worth from what we do rather than from who we are. One of the strategies of God to help this process along is to allow some of the 'props' that we depend on for self-worth and security to be removed from our lives, thus taking away those things from which we get a false sense of identity. We are then free to find our security, self-worth and significance in God alone.

This again can happen in a number of ways, but it often involves loss in some form. We are left exposed and inadequate as we see that our trust was not in Christ at all, but in some other person or object. These tests of faith come in various shapes and sizes—redundancy, business failure, marriage break-up, illness, financial hardship, relationship difficulties, unfair criticism, transition and change—the list is endless. You will know what it means for you. It is not so much that God causes these things to happen as that when they do come our way, he uses them to show us things about ourselves that we may not otherwise realize. Each time something is taken from us, it reveals where our security really lies.

I have just been through a time of severe trial. The church that I lead experienced a sudden loss of members, and, being small already, we were fighting for our very existence. I took it quite badly because some of those who left us were personal friends of long standing. As I asked God, 'Why?' I could only see that he was pruning us as a church, and that he was testing my character. Was my self-worth rooted in leading a successful church, or was it in Christ alone? Did I have the strength of character to keep going, or would I quit and call it a day? It was a searching time for me, and I have only made it by God's grace. I hope that I have become stronger as a result of this experience, able to bear more fruit in days to come because some of my inner motivations have been refined and purified.

Neither cleansing nor pruning are 'fun' times. They reveal the determination of the divine gardener to produce in our lives a crop of fruit that will glorify his name. The more we desire to glorify him, the more we will be tested. We may not welcome the testing, but we know it is the only way to bear fruit, and so we willingly submit to God's gracious dealings in our lives.

God deals with each of us as individuals, just as the vine dresser treats each branch separately. God has a purpose for your life, and his activity in your life will be shaped according to that purpose. God will prune you according to your needs, and so that your life will better fulfil his unique plan for you. No two people are alike in this respect. Always he deals with us tenderly and carefully, acting out of his wisdom and in love. 'Always remember,' says Selwyn Hughes, 'that no matter how often the secateurs snip, or how painful the pruning, your life is in good hands: it is your *Father* who is the Gardener.'[17]

✣

My hands were full—
Both of useful, necessary things,
And of broken, sentimental things
Kept from habit.
Clutter I clung to,
Giving it value
It did not merit

He said: 'There is more
But first you must loosen your grip'—
And He took what I'd held to so tightly:
My dear treasure.
Empty I waited,
Mourning my losses
Tears without measure.

So I was ready.
And into the sad aching void
There poured a new blessing, undreamt of:
A glad tomorrow.
Priceless bounty
I could not have held
Until my hands had let go.

BARBARA PARSONS

QUESTIONS FOR REFLECTION

For individuals

1. How is the idea of the 'seasons of the soul' helpful to you? Can you identify which season you are currently in?
2. What are the two reasons for pruning? How has God used his word to 'clean up' your own life? Why do we sometimes still experience a battle with temptation?
3. How do you understand God's discipline, and why is it an act of love? Review any times when you have experienced his loving discipline. What happened? What did you learn?
4. What do you understand by pruning for growth? Why is it essential? In the light of this, review again (a) your 'religious activism', and (b) the sources of your identity outside of Christ.
5. Do you have a spiritual director or mentor? Why might this be helpful? How could you find such a person?

For groups

1. Summarize together the different phases or seasons in the spiritual life. If possible, share individually which season you feel you may be in just now. What do you sense that God is doing in your life?
2. Why is cleansing important to fruitfulness? How does God use his word to achieve this? Why do we not believe in sinless perfection?
3. In what ways does God discipline his people, and why? What lessons can we learn from the church at Corinth? Why is a healthy fear of the Lord desirable?
4. What do we mean by 'spiritual pruning'? Why is religious activism a danger? How might this apply to a church?
5. What provision can a church make to help individuals maintain a close walk with God?

THE SECRET OF THE VINE:
THE KEY TO EVERYTHING

9

ABIDING

Remain in me, and I will remain in you. No branch can bear fruit by itself; it must remain in the vine. Neither can you bear fruit unless you remain in me (v. 4).

We began our study of John 15 by considering the importance of bearing fruit for God. We have seen how, by means of the allegory of the vine and its branches, Jesus described the intimate relationship between himself, the Father, and those who believe. We have also considered the ways in which the divine gardener works to ensure that this is a healthy and productive relationship. We now come to the heart of the matter: the importance of abiding in Christ.

The verse we are looking at contains the main point of the allegory. Just as it impossible for a branch to bear fruit by itself, so we cannot bear the kind of fruit that lasts, and which glorifies God, unless we learn to abide in him. Jesus is stressing here the absolute necessity of a close, living relationship with himself as the only way to live the Christian life effectively. We must therefore take time to consider what it means to 'abide in Christ'.

The NIV chooses to use the word 'remain' in this context, a more functional word than 'abide', which was used in the King James Version, and which has slipped more comfortably into Christian vocabulary. In some ways they mean exactly the same, but perhaps the word 'remain' reminds us that God has placed us into Christ, and that is where we are to stay or continue. When we speak about abiding in Christ, we are not to think of a condition that we have to attain, but rather of a state which already exists, and which has only to be continued.

It is one of the wonders of conversion that God has, by his own initiative and grace, taken us out of our old identity 'in Adam' and placed us 'in Christ', thereby giving us a brand new identity (see Romans 5:12–21). This happens at the moment of our new birth. 'To be born again,' says Scottish minister James Philip, 'is to be born into Christ, into union with him.'[18] A supernatural joining takes place, whereby we are made one with Christ. Paul explained it like this. 'But he who unites himself with the Lord is one with him in spirit' (1 Corinthians 6:17).

This, then, is the starting point of the Christian life, a fact of our new relationship to God, and something we can assume and build upon. It is nothing to do with how we feel or what we have achieved. It is a position that has been granted to us. We are already 'in Christ' and all we have to do is stay there, becoming increasingly aware of our new identity, growing daily in the consciousness of who we are in him. To abide in Christ, therefore, at its most basic level, is simply to remember that this is our true position and to live in the light of it.

The word 'abide', however, is a much deeper word than 'remain', and brings out another facet of the Greek word (*meno*) that is used here. To 'abide' is to make our home somewhere, to find a dwelling place where we can rest and feel that we belong. It carries with it the idea of tarrying as a guest, of lodging somewhere, of having a place to live. It is not difficult to see that Jesus is inviting us to make our home in him, to allow him to become our resting place, to make him the focus of our lives.

It is often said that 'home is where the heart is', and it is to this kind of intimacy that we are called. This thought is very dominant throughout the writings of the apostle John, for he speaks of 'abiding' at least 40 times in his Gospel, and 26 times in his letters. It is captured in the promise of Jesus: 'If anyone loves me, he will obey my teaching. My Father will love him, and we will come to him and make our home with him' (John 14:23).

The expression 'to set up home together' is sometimes used figuratively of getting married, and of course the relationship between Christ and the church is often described in those terms (see Ephesians 5:22–33). Paul says that this is a profound mystery, but suggests that as two people become one flesh in the marriage relationship, so there is an intimate union between Christ and his church, and between him and each individual believer. We may not understand this with our minds, but in our hearts it is wonderfully possible to begin to grow into oneness with Jesus, and to have a deepening sense of being united with him in a strong, satisfying love relationship.

All this lies behind the thought of abiding in Christ. Yes, it is a fact of our new life in Christ, and not dependent on emotional experiences; but it is also an experiential reality that we can feel and know. And as we shall see later on, it is out of this relationship that a life of maximum fruitfulness becomes possible.

There is one final thought locked up within the word 'abide'. As well as referring to a position we already enjoy, or a place where we love to be, it carries with it the thought of spending time with someone—the suggestion that to abide is to linger, to rest, to wait. Thus, in the story of the Emmaus road, the disciples encourage the risen Jesus, 'Stay (*meno*) with us, for it is nearly evening; the day is almost over' (Luke 24:29). And, of course, he went in to stay, to abide, with them.

The two words 'union' and 'communion' are often placed together, and the second is the natural outcome of the first. Those who experience the oneness of 'union' can most easily deepen that into the joy of 'communion', and indeed the goal of union is to make communion possible. Why has God placed us into Christ? So that we may know him in an ever-deepening oneness, experiencing friendship and fellowship with him, and taking time to enjoy each other.

Hudson Taylor, the great missionary to China, wrote in 1894 a little booklet based on the Song of Songs, which he took to be an allegory of the love relationship between Christ and the believer. He called his booklet *Union and Communion*. He wanted to share with others the wonderful truth that he had discovered for himself: that it is possible, despite the ups and downs in our relationship with Jesus, to find in him a life of deep satisfaction. He wrote:

Union with Christ, and abiding in Christ, what do they not secure? Peace, perfect peace; rest, constant rest; answers to all our prayers; victory over all our foes; pure, holy living; ever-increasing fruitfulness. All these are the glad outcome of abiding in Christ. To deepen this union, to make more constant this abiding, is the practical use of this precious Book.[19]

If this sounds idealistic and romantic, remember that it came from the pen of a man who, through a lifetime of gritty service in China, accomplished a great work for God in the face of many trials and adversities, and who was not given to exaggeration or sentimentality.

Perhaps, in our activity-dominated lives, we have forgotten what it is to linger in the presence of Jesus. Perhaps, in our desire to achieve external goals, we have neglected the development of our inner life—less measurable, but much more vital. Maybe we are more used to living on the surface of life than to plumbing its depths. It takes time to abide in Christ, and there are no short cuts to the kind of intimacy of which Taylor wrote, and to which Jesus is inviting us.

It is clear from the words of Jesus here that 'abiding' is not something passive. 'Remain in me' carries with it a sense of command, and seems to be a precursor to the second part of his statement, 'I will remain in you'. So how, in practical terms, are we to abide in Christ? If it is so central to our being fruitful for God and finding a life that satisfies, what steps can we take to make it a reality?

It is generally accepted that we abide in Christ by our practice of what are called the 'spiritual disciplines'. A spiritual discipline is any action we take that expresses our dependency on God and enables us to live from his divine resources. They are the practical means by which his life is allowed to flow into our lives. The use of the word 'discipline' reminds us that these are 'holy habits', patterns of behaviour that we cultivate because they help us to achieve our goal of knowing Christ more fully. They are not rules or regulations that we slavishly obey, but helpful activities that bring us to the place where we can receive more grace into our lives.

Abiding in Christ does not just happen; we discipline ourselves to stay close to him, and choose to behave in ways that draw us nearer to him. The disciplines are not the life; they merely make it possible for us to receive the life. As Richard Foster helpfully puts it, 'A farmer is helpless to grow grain; all he can do is provide the right conditions for the growing of grain. He puts the seed in the ground where the natural forces take over and up comes the grain. That is the way with the Spiritual Disciplines—they are a way of sowing to the Spirit.'[20]

What, then, are these disciplines? Foster himself divides them under three headings. First, he identifies the inward disciplines of meditation, prayer, study and fasting; next, the outward disciplines of simplicity, solitude, submission and service. Finally, he lists the corporate disciplines of confession, worship, guidance and celebration. We are not, of course, expected to practise all of these at the same time, and with full intensity! Each one of them in itself can be a vehicle to draw us into greater intimacy with God. It is more a question of knowing which discipline will be most helpful to us at a particular time, and to be open to the full variety of spiritual practice that they represent.

A more recent writer on the disciplines is American professor and Baptist minister Dallas Willard. His definition of a spiritual discipline is 'an activity undertaken to bring us into more effective co-operation with Christ and his Kingdom', and he says that they are undertaken 'to make us capable of receiving more of his life and power'.[21] Willard divides the disciplines into two categories. The 'Disciplines of Abstinence' he names as solitude, silence, fasting, frugality, chastity, secrecy and sacrifice. The 'Disciplines of Engagement' he gives as study, worship, celebration, service, prayer, fellowship, confession and submission. Willard himself says that there is no complete list of disciplines, nor should we assume that our particular list will be suitable for others. It is a question of deciding which spiritual practices work best for us as individuals, and then incorporating them into our lifestyles. We must always remember that they are not an end in themselves. It is not the practice of the disciplines that is important, but abiding more fully in Christ.

I do not intend to describe the disciplines in detail, although we will look later at some practical ways of abiding in Christ that are suggested by what Jesus says in this passage. My purpose here is mainly to point out the active nature of abiding, and to encourage those who have a hunger for greater intimacy with Jesus to look for creative ways to do this, and not merely to sit back in a passive state of super-spirituality.

I was brought up to have a regular 'quiet time'. This I understood to be the daily practice of reading the Bible (with the help of suitable explanatory notes) and prayer (with the help of a prayer diary). This is a tried and tested formula, but the danger is that we forget why we are doing it. All too easily the goal of the quiet time becomes to complete the day's reading and then hurry off to more pressing activities, or to pray through the items, ticking off the requests in the same way as we might with our shopping list. We lose sight of the bigger picture: that the purpose of a quiet time is to spend time with God, to be drawn into greater intimacy with his Son, and to position ourselves once again in the place of abiding.

How different my own 'quiet times' have become since I re-discovered the bigger picture! Now I realize that the goal is to meet with a person—Jesus, the lover of my soul. Now I am happy to linger in his presence, soaking up his love, often without spoken words, sometimes with the help of gentle music. When I read the scriptures, it is so that I might find him and remind myself of who I am in him. When I pray, it is out of a consciousness of my oneness with him, and a sharing of his heart.

This starting point has become my 'home base'. I want my life to be lived out of this place of abiding in Christ. He is the source of my life, and it is natural to want to begin the day by drawing upon his resources. The disciplines add variety to my basic daily routine, and variety is the spice of life. They enable me to encounter Jesus in fresh ways, to revitalize my walk with him, to add greater depth and reality to my relationship with him.

I cannot over-emphasize the importance or the joy of learning to abide in Christ. Not only is it the way to greater fruitfulness, but it is also the way to greater satisfaction and fulfilment in the Christian life. If you find that the sparkle has gone out of your walk with God, that Christian living has become a burden and service a lifeless chore, it may be that you need to discover the wonder of a life lived out of intimacy with Jesus.

Home is a safe place—
It is where you are best known
And best loved;
Most welcome.

The world is not home—
It will use you and fool you;
Manipulate,
Reject you.

Jesus is your home,
A safe place to hide you;
Celebrate you
Accept you.

Let the Father take you home.
BARBARA PARSONS

10

THE *BIG* LESSON

If a man remains in me and I in him, he will bear much fruit; apart from me you can do nothing (v. 5).

The necessity of abiding in Christ is again brought home to us in this verse. Why do we need to abide? Because *apart from him we can do nothing.* Separated from Jesus we are cut off from the source of our life, and we can no longer bear fruit. Connected to him we receive his divine life, and fruit-bearing is the natural outcome. Abiding is therefore essential.

There is, however, one issue that hinders our abiding in Christ, and that is our natural tendency to want to do things ourselves. This principle of 'independence' is actually at the root of all sin, for sin—whatever form it takes—is essentially about living independently of God. Human pride is the outward expression of this independent attitude, and it exists in all of us, for it is the legacy of the fall. Even after we are converted, we still exhibit the same tendency to independent living and to depending on what the Bible often calls 'the flesh'.

Although it is a term used in many different ways, 'the flesh' often refers to the techniques and strategies we employ to get our needs met outside of God. It describes the way in which we choose to live apart from God, depending on our own resources and strength. Although we are created to live in dependency on God, and to receive our life from him, we have chosen to live separately and to depend on ourselves to get by.

Even after conversion, we have a tendency to operate in the same way, seeking to do God's work from our own strength, depending upon our own natural human abilities. The flesh, to our surprise, can be very religious! We find ourselves trying in our own strength to please God, doing his will out of our own resources, instead of depending upon him to work in us and through us.

Some people, for instance, are very conscientious and responsible, and they begin to live the Christian life with a great sense of duty and obligation. Without realizing it, they begin to operate out of their own strength, feeling that everything depends upon them, and that they are responsible for making things happen. Of course they ask God for help, but the burden of responsibility is on their shoulders, and they feel it very greatly. Essentially, they are doing the work, and God is helping them, but it remains their work. No wonder the Christian life seems hard and demanding, and such people often feel exhausted and drained. This is not how God intended us to operate. The work is his, and he made us to live in dependency upon him, allowing him to work in us and through us. Dependency and abiding are meant to go together.

There are as many sources of human strength as there are individuals. We each have our own unique way of operating apart from God, and we have each developed our own unique 'flesh patterns'—ways of achieving things by ourselves. Some people depend on their intellectual abilities and powers of persuasion, others on their will-power and determination. Some are very talented and have many natural gifts; others are resourceful and ingenious. Some rely on their charm and personality, others on pleasing people and being popular. It is important that, as individuals, we become aware of the ways in which we are tempted to act independently of God, and ask for discernment about the sources of our own natural strength. We need to know what our own 'flesh patterns' look like.

It is exactly at this point that we begin to learn what I have called 'the *big* lesson'. I call it 'big' because of its significance, and because of its impact upon us. If we are to bear fruit from God, sooner or later we will have to learn that 'apart from me you can do nothing'.

It is a lesson that cuts right across our natural strength and our tendency to operate out of our 'flesh'. For this reason it is often a painful lesson, and one that may involve a crisis, as well as a process.

In order to bring us to a place of dependency upon him, God has to weaken our own natural strength. As long as we think we can do it, albeit with a little help from God, we will be operating out of natural strength, and that can never glorify God. He has to show us that we cannot bear fruit that glorifies him by ourselves. He will therefore allow to come into our lives those circumstances that will bring us to a point of weakness, revealing our absolute need of him and our total inability to achieve spiritual results apart from him. This is what we might call God's 'severe mercy'. We can be sure that it is part of his agenda for each of us, and that somehow, in the circumstances of our own lives, he will be working towards this end.

God has many ways of bringing us to this place of brokenness. He may allow us to fail in some way, either in the sense of not achieving our cherished goals, or of not being able to live up to our own ideals. We may suffer burnout or exhaustion before we realize that our own strength is insufficient. Some may have to experience painful times of disappointment and disillusionment before they come to the end of themselves. Others may experience physical weakness and limitation that curbs their natural energy and enthusiasm. However he achieves it, God's goal is always to bring us to a place of dependency upon himself, where we realize that we cannot do the work without him.

Dr Raymond Edman, at the time President of Wheaton College in America, did a study of the lives of 20 different people who had experienced a dramatic change in their lives and ministries, reflecting the way in which God deals with us along these lines. He summed up his findings in this way: 'The pattern seems to be: self-centredness, self-effort, increasing inner dissatisfaction and outer discouragement, a temptation to give it all up because there is no better way; and then finding the Spirit of God to be their strength, their guide, their confidence and companion—in a word, their life.'[22]

American writer Steve McVey tells how God taught him this crucial lesson in his pastoral ministry. He had moved from a very successful church in Alabama to a new situation in Atlanta, Georgia. Armed with his best sermons and proven church growth programmes, he anticipated a similar successful ministry in the new situation, but try as he might, he could not reproduce the same results. For the first time in 17 years of ministry he saw his church in decline. Tired and empty, he poured his frustrations out to God. 'Lord,' he said, 'I'm tired of struggling for victory in my own life and I am tired of striving for success in my ministry.'

Late one night, at the height of his crisis and in his utter brokenness, he surrendered himself afresh to God, choosing to lay aside the things that he had previously relied upon—his efforts to have a growing church, his hunger for affirmation in ministry, his education and experience. Through his failure, God was bringing him to an end of self-sufficiency.

It was several months later that Steve began to realize the reason for his failure and what God was doing in his life. He began to understand 'the *big* lesson' that God was teaching him—that by himself he could do nothing. He began to realize that Christ was to be the source of his life, and that he had to learn to allow Jesus to live his life through him. It was a turning-point in his life, and marked the beginning of a whole new phase of fruitful ministry that has impacted many people around the world as he has shared the message of what is often called 'the exchanged life'.[23]

We have already mentioned Hudson Taylor, the great missionary pioneer whose life has influenced so many worldwide, not only through his work in China but through the example of his life. He was also one who came to know through painful experience that he could bear no lasting fruit for God without abiding in Christ. The story of how he came to experience the 'exchanged life' (the expression seems to have originated with him) is well-known, and is recorded in *Hudson Taylor's Spiritual Secret*, written by his son and daughter-in-law.

Taylor had already been working in China for 16 years, and had founded his own missionary society, the China Inland Mission. In the months leading up to his crisis experience, he went through many days of deep darkness. Not only were there political troubles affecting the work in China, but there was disaffection among some of the newly recruited workers. Financial constraints added to the strains upon him, as did constant battles with health problems. Trials surrounded him on every side, but it was the inner struggle that concerned him most. He longed for a deeper personal holiness for himself and the other members of the mission, and yet was constantly aware of his own shortcomings, particularly his irritability and lack of patience. God was at work in his life, weakening his natural strength, although he little realized it at the time.

The breakthrough came eventually in the form of a letter from a friend, John McCarthy, describing his own recent experience of learning to abide in Christ. Taylor recognized at once that this was the answer to the longing of his own heart, and in that moment, as he read, he saw it all clearly. He later wrote to his sister, 'The Spirit of God revealed to me the truth of our *oneness with Jesus* as I had never known it before.'[24] He had long been aware that if only he could abide in Christ, all would be well, but he did not know how, and personal discipline and trying harder made no difference. Now he saw that it was simply a matter of faith, of accepting the truth of his position in Christ and the reality that he needed only to abide in him as a branch abides in the vine.

As I thought of the Vine and the branches, what light the blessed Spirit poured direct into my soul! How great seemed my mistake in wishing to get the sap, the fullness, out of Him! I saw not only that Jesus will never leave me, but that I am a member of His body, of His flesh and of His bones. The vine is not the root merely, but all—root, stem, branches, twigs, leaves, flowers, fruit. And Jesus is not that alone—He is soil and sunshine, air and showers, and ten thousand times more than we have ever dreamed, wished for or needed. Oh the joy of seeing this truth![25]

A period of crisis followed by a moment of revelation—this seems to have been the way by which this great man of God was brought to a life-changing encounter. From that time onward, despite increasing trials and difficulties, he continued to enjoy a deep intimacy with God and a life of increasing fruitfulness. He had learned the *big* lesson, that apart from Christ he could do nothing, but with him all things were possible.

Humanly speaking,
Growing up has to do with
Learning to become
Self-sufficient,
Successful,
Independent.

Spiritual growth
Is Jesus filling my whole being,
And my absolute
Childlike
Dependency.
BARBARA PARSONS

11

WITHERED BRANCHES?

If anyone does not remain in me, he is like a branch that is thrown away and withers; such branches are picked up, thrown into the fire and burned (v. 6).

Imagine this if you can. A branch has been snapped off the vine, and is lying discarded on the ground. What does it look like? What will happen to it? Well, at first it looks just as it always did when it was attached to the vine, but gradually, after a short time, changes begin to appear. The leaves start to curl at the edges, and the skin of the grapes wrinkles. Eventually the leaves lose their greenness, and become yellow and dry. The fruit grows wizened and shrunken. The wood itself is brittle and easily broken. As far as the vine dresser is concerned, it has no further use. It is fit only to be used as kindling for the fire.

What Jesus is describing here is what happens when a believer fails to abide in him and loses that life-giving contact with the one who is their Saviour. Their inner life begins to wither, their spiritual vitality begins to wane. For a while we may not detect any difference, but gradually the effects will be seen. Perhaps they lose their joy or their peace. Maybe their attendance at church begins to drop off, and their desire for fellowship decreases. They might lose their appetite for the word of God, or opt out of Christian service. Prayer becomes difficult, worship seems a chore. They may begin to spend their money on material things, and give their time to pleasure-seeking rather than to spending time with God. Perhaps some of their old ways return, and sins that they had left behind begin to reassert themselves. Gradually, they become unproductive and unfruitful, simply because they have ceased to draw their life and strength from the one who is the source of their life. It can happen so easily and so subtly. This is a warning that we all need to hear.

We must remember, though, that this is an allegory, and in an allegory not every detail has an application. In understanding an allegory, it is important to keep to the main point of the illustration, and not to read into it things that the speaker never intended. In scripture, any allegory must be interpreted also in the light of the rest of the teaching of the Bible. Jesus is seeking to emphasize the necessity of abiding in him and the consequences of failing to do so. He is not saying that those who fail to abide will somehow be punished or lose their salvation. That would be to push the illustration too far, and run counter to the rest of scripture. He is reminding us that if we fail to abide, we will 'wither' spiritually and become unfruitful and unproductive. That is painful enough.

Why do people fail to abide in Christ? The most common reason is because they are too busy. As we have seen already, it takes time to abide in Christ, and time is not something we have much of in our hectic, frantic lives. Of course, we all have the same amount of time, but we choose to use it differently. With so many demands upon us, we have to be able to recognize our priorities so that we can give our time to what is most important to us. The sad reality is that many of us do not regard time to nurture our inner lives as a priority. It is more often considered a luxury, something we will do if we get round to it. The trouble is that with so many demands on us, we seldom do get round to it. The tyranny of the urgent always seems to rule our lives, and we are poorer as a result. God is squeezed out to the margins of our lives, instead of being at the centre.

Even for those in Christian ministry, the temptation is very real to be so busy doing things for God that we neglect to spend time with him. Mike Pilavachi, who is pastor of Soul Survivor, the well-known youth church in Watford, tells how he was deeply affected by a written sermon preached nearly 50 years ago by Duncan

Campbell, a Scottish minister at the heart of the Hebridean revival. Campbell was warning of the danger of replacing fellowship with God with activity, saying that 'many a Christian worker has buried his spirituality in the grave of his activity'.

Pilavachi says that this sentence went through him like a knife. 'We so often kid ourselves that God is pleased with us on the basis of what we achieve,' he writes, 'when the fact is he wants our fellowship more than he wants our work.' He goes on to add that in a world where success is based on results, 'our great need is to understand that being is better than, and precedes, doing. Indeed activity that does not come from being in His presence is a waste of time and effort.'[26]

The oft-repeated, but seldom heeded, warning of 'the barrenness of a busy life' is very real. Those of us who have grown up with an active spirituality, and who by personality are more extravert, are the most at risk. We find ourselves drawn into an ever-increasing spiral of well-intentioned activity that eventually drains the life out of us. Our zeal for serving God becomes the very thing that prevents us from knowing him more deeply and personally, and from learning how to let him do his work through us. We substitute human enthusiasm for divine life, and wonder why the results are so meagre.

If busyness represents one of the main obstacles to abiding in Christ, a second and closely related danger is that of caring for others and neglecting ourselves. This is a danger that can seem so noble, even 'Christian', and it is a trap into which many fall unwittingly. It particularly affects those in the helping professions and those who have the welfare of others on their hearts. Their concern for others is so great that they forget about themselves, and sometimes about their own relationship with God.

It is, of course, quite right 'to give and not to count the cost',[27] at least to a degree. This sentiment keeps us from slothful ease and reminds us that Christian service is a costly business. Sometimes we must sacrifice our time and put the needs of others before our own. Sometimes we are called upon to give up our 'rights' (to privacy, rest, material comfort, leisure, relationships and so on), and we can do so gladly and willingly for the sake of Christ. Yet the other side of the coin is that if we do not look after ourselves as well, eventually we will have nothing more to give to others. We shall find ourselves burnt out, drained of life, bankrupt of compassion. Then who can we help?

Clearly there is a need for balance. I cannot give the water of life to others if my own well is dry; and if I neglect my inner life because of my duty to others I may eventually pay a heavy price. In order to help others, I must ensure that I am receiving into my own life the divine resources on which such compassionate ministry depends. In other words, I must take time to abide in Christ and receive from him, in order that I can minister life to the needy.

No one was more compassionate than Henri Nouwen, yet he was clear on this point.

We serve the world by being spiritually well. The first question is not 'How much do we do?' or 'How many people do we help out?' but 'Are we interiorly at peace?' The distinction between contemplation and action can be misleading. Jesus' actions flowed from his interior communion with God. His presence was healing, and it changed the world. In a sense he didn't do anything! 'Everyone who touched him was healed.' [28]

Confusion over this point has caused many to 'wither' in their spiritual lives, simply because they felt guilty at taking time aside from the needs of others. Such false guilt has to be resisted, however. We are not being selfish or indulgent when we give time to being with Jesus. If he truly is the source of our life, then it is inconceivable that we should do anything less. We can only love others with the love that he gives, and that is why it is so important that we continue to abide in him despite the ever-present needs of those around us.

I find personally that a third danger is just as insidious in the way it can draw me away from God, and it concerns my response to pressure. It is easy to spend time with God when the world is at peace and everything is in harmony, but when something comes along to disrupt the equilibrium, I find I can easily be led away from the place of abiding into a period of straining and striving. I suppose it is a normal human response to stress that we want to do something about it. When problems surface and difficulties arise, we want to take charge, move into action, sort it out. Before we know it, self-effort has taken over, and we are operating again out of the 'flesh'—in this case the need to be in control.

If the pressures are very great, panic sets in and fear grips our hearts. We find it difficult to concentrate, and prayer becomes difficult. It seems almost impossible to abide in Christ, for our minds wander and, like a guided missile, seem to lock on to the problems we are facing. Our minds become filled with worry, our bodies racked with anxiety, and our spirits weighed down with care. We lose our peace and joy, and our effectiveness diminishes. We forget our identity in Christ and all sense of proportion is gone.

At such times we need to remember that our place in Christ is secure and not dependent upon our feelings. We can abide in Christ whether we feel it or not, and we accept the fact of our oneness with Christ regardless of our circumstances. It is also at such times that the spiritual disciplines come into their own. These 'holy habits' that we have already identified, which we need to build into our lives, must continue regardless of our feelings. We stick to the basic disciplines of our walk with God despite our emotions. Sometimes it is a matter of gritting our teeth, holding on and waiting for the storm to pass.

Each time this happens, we are learning how to deal with our fears and worries more effectively in days to come. As we grow and mature, we will become more rooted in Christ and less easily destabilized by our circumstances. The more Christ has become our 'home', the less easily Satan will be able to entice us away from our place of rest.

This is not an exhaustive list of the hindrances to abiding in Christ, but these are the most common problems. Sin, if indulged and not confronted, will always cause a restriction in the flow of

God's life to us, and if our hearts get attached to other things rather than Christ, this will also damage our inner life. Ignorance of the importance of abiding, and of the practical steps that make it a reality, is a factor for some. Others feel unworthy, and can hardly believe that such a relationship of intimacy is possible, or at least not for them.

Most of us find that our abiding is imperfect and long for a greater consistency in our walk with God. The good news is that, unlike a branch that has been broken off, we can be reconnected, and our fellowship with Jesus can be easily restored. It only requires that we turn our hearts again towards him in repentance and faith.

I like to joke with my friends that I was born in the years BC— that is, before computers! I can just about manage to use the new technology, but if I have a problem I usually need to consult my children, for whom computers and the internet are second nature. So recently, when my computer 'died' on me, I called my daughter for help.

'Dad,' she said, 'always remember one thing with computers. If something goes wrong, first of all check the connections.'

This I dutifully did, and discovered to my relief that one of the connections was indeed loose. It was easily sorted, and the problem solved. The computer just needed to be reconnected.

Surely there is a lesson for us here. If we feel that our spiritual lives are going wrong, and our walk with God is no longer satisfying or rewarding, what should we do? Check the connections! Have we lost our place of abiding? Have we allowed our intimacy with Jesus to slip? Have we been guilty of drifting away or of losing contact? It is easily sorted. All we need to do is return to the Lord and reestablish that living relationship once again. We may need to let go of certain things and make some adjustments, but that will not be difficult if we consider the joy of being restored to fellowship once more.

✣

An axe is as useful
As the man who wields it;

A paintbrush as skilful
As the artist who guides it;

A story as intriguing
As the one who tells it;

Axe, brush, story
Such potential—
The skill of the master,
Essential.

So a branch is as fruitful
As the vine that bears it.

Cut off, it lies waste,
It withers and dies—
All its potential
Unrealised.

BARBARA PARSONS

QUESTIONS FOR REFLECTION

For individuals

1. What do you understand by the term 'abiding', and why is it the key to everything?
2. What practical steps can we take to help us abide? Which of the spiritual disciplines do you currently use? Which of them are you unfamiliar with? Might these new ones prove helpful?
3. How has God been teaching you the *big* lesson of dependency? What ways of independent living ('flesh patterns') do you think you have? What can you do about them?
4. Why do you sometimes fail to abide? How can you tell when you are not abiding, and what are the spiritual consequences?
5. How is abiding in Christ linked to fruitfulness? Given the active nature of abiding in Christ, what do you think you will now do to turn the fact of your 'union' with Christ into the experience of 'communion'?

For groups

1. What does it mean to abide in Christ, and why is it important for us to do so?
2. How do you understand the term 'spiritual disciplines'? Why is it important to develop these 'holy habits'?
3. What is the *big* lesson that God tries to teach us? What ways does he commonly use to show us our need to depend on him?
4. How might 'the flesh' (the independent self) show itself? Why can we speak of 'religious flesh'? How does God deal with 'the flesh'?
5. What are the three most common reasons that people fail to abide in Christ? What effect does this have on their spiritual life? How can we maintain our place of abiding in Christ?

THE LIFE OF THE VINE: RECEIVING THE 'SAP'

12

THE DISCIPLINE OF DEPENDENCY

No branch can bear fruit by itself (v. 4)… apart from me you can do nothing (v. 6).

The beautiful island of Madeira lies just off the coast of Portugal. Famous for its stunning scenery, its magnificent flowers and luxuriant vegetation, this popular tourist destination has one problem: most of the rain falls in the mountainous centre of the island, while most of its people live on the sunny coastal fringe. To transport the water from where it falls to where it is most needed, the Madeiran people have cut out of the hillsides mile after mile of irrigation channels, known locally as *levadas*.

These *levadas* make splendid pathways for walkers, who love to follow their gentle descent towards the coast. Clinging to the mountains and following the contours slowly downward, the carefully constructed channels provide breathtaking panoramic views of the island as they guide the life-giving supply of water to the farms and houses of the drier south. There, land that otherwise might be dry and barren is transformed into the delightful subtropical paradise that attracts visitors from all over the world.

Levadas are a wonderful picture to me of the spiritual disciplines about which we have already spoken. These 'holy habits' are the channels by which God's life is communicated to us. They are the means by which the sap is able to reach the branches. They are not an end in themselves, but they make it possible for the life of Jesus to flow freely into our lives.

We turn our attention now to the five key disciplines that emerge from our study of this passage, by which we can maintain our place of abiding in Christ. The first is what I call the discipline of dependency, and it arises from our awareness of the truth of what Jesus is saying here—that apart from him we can do nothing. If I understand this truth to any degree, it will cause me to live in dependency upon God and, seeing him as the source of my life, to seek to derive all my strength and motivation from him alone.

We were created to live in dependency upon God, but sin—the emergence of the independent self—destroyed that trusting relationship. Pride caused humankind to want to live without reference to God, to do their own thing. Repentance, which restores the relationship with God, is essentially a turning away from this independent lifestyle and a turning towards a life that is once again dependent upon God. None of us finds this easy, since it is a humbling process, but by one means or another, God seeks to guide us back to the place of dependency.

Long ago, King Solomon spoke of this same principle. 'Unless the Lord builds the house, its builders labour in vain. Unless the Lord watches over the city, the watchmen stand guard in vain' (Psalm 127:1).

Some people are builders by nature. They see the possibilities of what might be, and have visions for the future. They want to achieve something for God. Such people are often strong natural leaders, with enthusiasm, above-average ability and lots of determination and will-power. They can make things happen, and, if we are this kind of person, therein lies the danger—that of relying on our own strength rather than on God. As Solomon reminds us, though, if we labour in our own strength we will not build anything that lasts or glorifies God. We may achieve a great deal as far as the human perspective is concerned, but from God's point of view it will be in vain.

Likewise, some people are care givers, who naturally watch over the lives of others. They want to encourage and support, to help others through their difficulties and be with them in their times of need. If we are a 'carer', this instinctive ability to feel for the needs of others means we are responsible, conscientious helpers, but the danger is that we tend to think that everything depends on us. We take the cares of the world on our shoulders. We try to do for others what only God himself can do, and if our counselling and comforting arise out of our own resources, then they will also be in vain.

It seems to be a human characteristic that when we are under pressure we try harder. Both 'builders' and 'carers' know what it is to go into overdrive in an attempt to maintain control or be successful. Solomon again reminds us that human energy will not accomplish the purpose of God: 'In vain you rise early and stay up late, toiling for food to eat—for he grants sleep to those he loves' (Psalm 127:2). The self-directed life is always full of stress and anxiety and produces very little. The God-dependent life, by contrast, is both fruitful and restful, for God takes the strain and he is the one who is responsible for making things happen.

How, then, can we know if we are living and working in God-dependency? Very simply—by the place that prayer has in our lives. If we know that without God's help we can achieve nothing of lasting spiritual worth, then our first recourse will be to prayer. Prayer is the means by which we open ourselves up to God and seek his help. In prayer we speak the language of dependency. It is essentially a cry for help, the soul's natural breath. It is the instinctive response of those who understand that by itself the branch can produce no fruit.

Answer this question for yourself honestly: what part does prayer play in your life? Is it foundational to all you do or is it a religious extra, tagged on to your life of busy activity? Is it really the air you breathe, or is it a reluctant concession to Christian practice, something you feel you ought to do? Is it a means of life to you, or is it simply something expected of you?

The discipline of dependency is expressed in a life of prayer, both the hidden life of personal prayer and the more public expression of corporate prayer. Prayer becomes the starting point for everything we do. There, in the secret place, we hear God speak to us, and receive direction for service and ministry. There we are refreshed and renewed as we wait upon God, and as we linger in his presence we are changed and transformed. Prayer becomes an essential, exciting, life-giving necessity.

Jesus himself provides us with a wonderful example of a God-dependent life. In the mystery of the incarnation he chose to empty himself of privileges associated with his equality with God and take human form, becoming a servant of all. The life he lived on earth he lived as a man, in complete dependency on God. This is why prayer was so important to him, and why his life was punctuated by periods of withdrawal, when he communed with his Father and received the sustenance he needed for the work he had been given to do. To our surprise we see that even Jesus could do nothing apart from the Father. Listen to his testimony:

The words I say to you are not just my own. Rather, it is the Father, living in me, who is doing his work (John 14:10).

When you have lifted up the Son of Man, then you will know that I am the one I claim to be and that I do nothing on my own but speak just what the Father has taught me (John 8:28).

I tell you the truth, the Son can do nothing by himself; he can do only what he sees his Father doing, because whatever the Father does the Son also does... By myself I can do nothing (John 5:19, 30).

Jesus' own life was a life of abiding in the Father, and he has set this as the pattern for all who follow him.

With this in mind, Jesus emphasized the centrality of prayer in the life of the believer. Early in his training of the disciples, he gave them (and us) this pertinent advice: 'Here's what I want you to do: Find a quiet, secluded place so you won't be tempted to role-play before God. Just be there as simply and honestly as you can manage. The focus will shift from you to God, and you will begin to sense his grace' (Matthew 6:6, THE MESSAGE). To do this, of course, we must be willing to cease all other activity in order to wait on God. Then the focus can shift from us to where it rightly belongs, on God.

The commands to 'stand still' and 'be still' are common in the Bible, and they express the need for human activity to cease so that divine activity may begin. It takes a great deal of courage and discipline to stop what you are doing and wait for God to act. Imagine Moses and the Israelites standing before the Red Sea with Pharaoh's armies closing in upon them. What panic he must have felt, and what pressure to do something, anything—build a bridge, dig a tunnel! Yet he was called to stand still and see the salvation of God, a God-dependent moment if ever there was one (Exodus 14:13–14).

At other times, depending on God can mean stepping out in faith, trusting that God will act as we respond to his leading. Like Joshua walking round the walls of Jericho, we are sometimes asked by God to express our dependency by doing something that moves us out of our comfort zone and places us in a position where, unless he acts, nothing will happen and we will be left looking foolish. The risk makes us depend even more upon him because we know that the situation is out of our control. At such moments, prayer is our only helpline.

Whether by standing still or stepping out, we learn that God is faithful and that, when we do depend upon him, he works on our behalf. It is both frightening and exhilarating to live in the discipline of dependency because it means that God is in control, and we are not. When we step aside and allow God to work in us and through us, we bear much fruit. Left to ourselves, we can struggle in our own strength and produce very little. Once we have submitted to the truth that 'apart from me you can do nothing', God is free to produce in us an abundant harvest that glorifies him because it has its origin in him.

✢

Air, water,
Warmth, food, shelter,
Are the necessities
On which my life depends.

Water,
Warmth, food and shelter
I can find for myself—
But not air.
Air must be provided for me,
Yet without it,
I most quickly die.

So with my life in Christ:
Prayer
Is the air
I breathe.

BARBARA PARSONS

13

THE DISCIPLINE OF SCRIPTURE

If you remain in me and my words remain in you…' (v. 7).

You will not find a direct reference to the Holy Spirit in the allegory of the vine, but he is there just the same. Although it remains unstated, I think we can safely say that the Holy Spirit is the 'sap' that flows between vine and branch, since it is the Spirit who communicates to us the life of God. The purpose of each of the spiritual disciplines is to allow us to receive this life-giving sap in order that we might be branches that bear fruit for God.

The scriptures are inspired by the Holy Spirit and, as such, contain the life of God. Paul said that all scripture is inspired by God (literally 'God-breathed'), and the systematic reading of the Bible is an obvious way by which we can tap into the life of God (2 Timothy 3:16). In these days of multimedia communication, when we prefer to see and hear information, fewer people read than ever before, and this can dramatically affect patterns of regular Bible reading. Nevertheless, it remains a key discipline for those who wish to abide in Christ and see their lives becoming productive for God.

Richard Taylor was a young man who had found himself in prison yet again. Sitting on the edge of his bed, he began to roll a cigarette, using for paper a page from the Gideon Bible that he had been given on admission. As he tore out a page at random, his eyes fell on the text. It was John chapter 1, and for some reason he began to read the words. To his surprise, he found that they spoke to him and he could not stop reading. As he read, he began to see his sinfulness, but also that Jesus could forgive him. There in his cell he gave his life to Christ, and today he is a minister of the gospel.[29]

Jesus said, 'The Spirit gives life; the flesh counts for nothing. The words I have spoken to you are spirit and they are life' (John 6:63). Time and again the Spirit of God has taken the written word and used it to speak of the living Word (Jesus) to those like Richard Taylor who feel that there is no hope. The scriptures have the unique ability to get right into our hearts, expose our need and show us how to find help. They plant within us the seed of new life, causing us to be born again (1 Peter 1:23). When we receive them as they really are—the word of God, not just human words—they begin to work in us, changing and transforming us (1 Thessalonians 2:13).

If we are to abide in Christ, we will need to soak ourselves in the scriptures. Paul encouraged his converts to let the word of Christ dwell in them richly (Colossians 3:16), or, as THE MESSAGE puts it, to let it 'have the run of the house'. The writer of Psalm 119 says similarly, 'I have hidden your word in my heart that I might not sin against you' (v. 11). The discipline of spending time in the word of God is a rewarding one, and there are a variety of ways by which we can do it.

It seems that in the early Church the public reading of scripture was a common practice, and Timothy is encouraged to devote himself to this custom (1 Timothy 4:13). It is still a good congregational discipline, but even more to be encouraged in our personal discipleship. I have found reading huge chunks of scripture at one sitting to be extremely helpful, for it has a way of cleansing and renewing the mind, causing our thoughts to become God-centred once again (Ephesians 5:26). Some schemes of reading can take us through the entire Bible in a year, and it is a great help to have this wider understanding of scripture. For those less ambitious, other programmes highlight the key passages in both Old and New Testaments and offer an overview of the whole Bible story, which is equally useful.[30] Sometimes, it can be refreshing to read through an entire Bible book at one sitting, and we have sometimes done this in a home group context. A few years ago, the Bible Society produced cassettes with a lively recording of the New Testament, encouraging those who were not so keen on reading to listen, either at home or as they travelled. Our church found this an excellent way to absorb the word of God. However we choose to do it, we need a greater exposure to scripture.

If reading provides the background for our understanding, concentrated study will help us to get the meaning of scripture, and gives us the tools to apply it to our daily lives. Again, Timothy is encouraged to 'study' diligently so that he can preach and teach accurately (2 Timothy 2:15, KJV). Here the use of commentaries and daily reading notes can be a great help, providing us with useful information and insights. Many churches run small groups for studying the scriptures together, and there are excellent materials available from a host of sources. The internet has opened up a wealth of resources too, with specialist sites providing access to teaching that would otherwise not be available. It is the truth that sets us free, and a proper understanding of the doctrines of the faith provides a strong platform for our experience to rest on.

Study is not an end in itself, however. There is always the danger that we forget why we are studying the Bible. Jesus warned the Pharisees of this danger: 'You diligently study the Scriptures because you think that by them you possess eternal life. These are the Scriptures that testify about me, yet you refuse to come to me to have life' (John 5:39–40). The issue is not 'How well do I know the Bible?' but 'Am I meeting with Jesus through my study?' The purpose of Bible study is to bring us closer to him so that we can abide in him and receive life from him. This is a perspective that we must not lose.

Added to our Bible reading and study, we can include scripture memorization. This is the main way in which we put the word of God into our hearts. I was fortunate that, as a young person, I was encouraged to memorize scripture. The Methodist chapel to which I belonged encouraged all the young people to take part in a district competition that included singing and Bible recitation. I can still remember the passages of scripture that I learned as a child, and ever since then I have found it fairly easy to remember key scriptures.

It is amazing how the Holy Spirit can bring those memorized scriptures to mind when we need them most. Once they are in our minds, they remain in our subconscious too, and can bring cleansing and healing even when we are not aware of it. Far better to have our minds filled with good thoughts than crammed with the messages with which the world bombards us. And when we have memorized scripture it is easy to engage in perhaps the most important activity of all—that of Bible meditation.

Bible meditation is the process of mentally 'chewing over' key verses or passages so that their truth can move from our heads to our hearts. As we think deeply over different words and phrases, the Holy Spirit can open our minds to their meaning and show us how to apply them to our lives. The process is well described by Bruce Wilkinson:

When you read your Bible, receive and savour it like food, like a treasure, like a love letter from God to you. Remember, you're reading in order to meet Someone. Ponder what you have read, and apply it to your present circumstances. Let it go down to the core of your being. And as you read, expect Him to commune with you.[31]

We should choose our passages for meditation carefully, so that they will have maximum benefit for us. Look for verses that speak about God's love for you, and your identity in Christ, for these are the most important truths to absorb. Find the scriptures that best meet your need at a given moment (if you are afraid or anxious and so on), and meditate on them as if they were words directly from Jesus to you. Be like Mary, and ponder them in your heart (Luke 2:19), or like Joshua, returning to them day and night (Joshua 1:8) until the truth grips you.

Once we have absorbed the truth into our hearts by meditation, it is helpful to turn it into spoken words, which we give back to

God in confession. This principle is taught in Romans 10:10 with regard to the assurance of salvation, which comes as we confess outwardly with our lips what God has already done in our hearts. 'For it is with your heart that you believe and are justified, and it is with your mouth that you confess and are saved.' This simple act of agreement with what God has said about us in his word is a powerful way of possessing the truth and making it actual in our experience.

I led a retreat where we had been meditating on the wonderful truth of 1 John 3:1 in order to help us experience the love of God: 'How great is the love the Father has lavished on us, that we should be called children of God! And that is what we are!' We savoured these words for several minutes, lingering over the key words and letting the truth of God's amazing love sink deep into our hearts. Then the time came for us to confess the truth we had been meditating upon. We chose to turn it into a personal prayer, something like this: 'Lord, I thank you that you are my Father and I am your child. I thank you for the greatness of your love, and for lavishing that love upon me. I rejoice that I am your son / daughter. That is who I really am. It is my true identity.' Many said that this simple act of confession, prayed out loud, was a liberating moment for them and a highlight of their retreat. We were abiding in Jesus by allowing his word to abide in us.

Like any of the disciplines, the discipline of scripture is not meant to bring us into legalistic bondage. We read and study as we are able, we memorize according to our ability, and we meditate because we want to. It is always important to ask God to create within us a hunger for himself and his word, and to help us find Jesus in that word. It is a deeper union with him that we seek, not just an increased knowledge of scripture.

✣

Some communications
Should be studied with the utmost care:
A map;
Battle orders;
A love letter.

Neglect to read a map
And you will lose your way;

Ignore battle orders
And you will suffer defeat;

Leave a love letter unread,
And you may never know
How greatly you are loved.

The Bible is God's communication to me.
Neglect it—I will lose my way.
Ignore it—I will be defeated.

Worst of all,
Unread,
I may never know
How greatly I am loved.

BARBARA PARSONS

14

THE DISCIPLINE OF
RECEIVING LOVE

As the Father has loved me, so have I loved you. Now remain in my love (v. 9).

It may seem strange to speak about the discipline of receiving love, but I believe it is appropriate. For many of us, allowing ourselves to be loved has to begin as a discipline, an act of faith. All Christians believe intellectually that God loves them, but few know it as a reality in their hearts. All too often we feel unworthy of God's love, and this deep-seated fear of not being good enough cripples many people in their walk with God. Here we are invited to make ourselves at home in the very love that we find so difficult to receive.

Jesus lived each moment of his earthly life within the circumference of the Father's love. He knew himself to be deeply loved by his *Abba* (Mark 14:36, Aramaic for 'daddy'), and this consciousness was the source of his strength throughout his life. The love relationship between Father and Son existed before his incarnation, for he was aware of being loved before the creation of the world (John 17:24). His coming to earth as a human being did nothing to change this love, but it did increase his need to be aware of it.

We find that twice during Jesus' time on earth, God spoke with a heavenly voice to remind him, and those listening, that he was indeed the beloved Son. At the Jordan river, during his baptism, a word of wonderful reassurance came as he began his earthly ministry: 'This is my Son, whom I love; with him I am well pleased' (Matthew 3:17). Before he had performed a miracle or delivered a sermon or done anything at all to deserve it, he was loved passionately by the Father. Then, as the cross drew near, a second moment of affirmation came. High up on the slopes of Mount Tabor, he was transfigured before his disciples and his true glory was fleetingly revealed. Most important of all, though, was the voice that spoke: 'This is my Son, whom I love; with him I am well pleased' (Matthew 17:5). No one seeing these things or hearing the voice could deny his true identity after that. Peter and those who saw it never forgot that sacred moment (2 Peter 1:17–18).

Throughout his ministry, the consciousness of his identity as the beloved remained with Jesus. He knew himself to be loved. 'The Father loves the Son,' he could confidently say (John 3:35; 5:20). This was the seal of approval upon him, the basis for his assurance (John 6:27). He made his home in the Father's love, and it was the place of his sustenance and strength. Now, as he speaks to his own disciples, he invites them into the circle of that love, to make their home there too by abiding in him and his love for them.

Amazingly, we are called to share in the warmth of the Father's unconditional love. He sings over us too a song of rapturous love, and we are urged to hear this song and live our lives to the rhythm of the heavenly melody. As the prophet said, 'He will take great delight in you, he will quiet you with his love, he will rejoice over you with singing' (Zephaniah 3:17). We too are called God's beloved, and his favour rests upon us. This is our identity as well.

Henri Nouwen tells movingly in *The Return of the Prodigal* how he discovered his true identity as a beloved child of God. It came as he meditated on the famous painting by Rembrandt depicting the story in Luke 16. 'Jesus made it clear to me,' he says, 'that the same voice that he heard at the River Jordan and on Mount Tabor can also be heard by me.'[32] For Nouwen, the far country is that place where we no longer hear the voice of love. We become the prodigal every time we seek for unconditional love outside of Christ—in being successful or popular or powerful, for example.

Home, on the other hand, is that place within us where we rest in the awareness of our belovedness and hear the Father say, 'You are my beloved, on you my favour rests.'

This wonderful book has helped many people to enter into their own experience of being the beloved, for this is true of all God's children. One of the main benefits of abiding in Christ is that it helps us to form our identity not in what we do, but in who we are. Brennan Manning puts it like this: 'God created us for union with Himself: This is the original purpose of our lives. And God is defined as love (1 John 4:16). Living in the awareness of our belovedness is the axis around which the Christian life revolves. Being the beloved is our identity, the core of our existence.'[33]

The apostle John had a particular revelation of this truth. His experience of leaning against Jesus during the Last Supper seems to have indelibly impressed upon him his identity as 'the disciple whom Jesus loved'. He could have defined himself as an apostle, a Gospel writer or a leader of the early Church. Instead, throughout his writings he introduces himself as the one whom Jesus loved (John 13:23; 19:26; 20:2; 21:7, 20). The exciting truth is that this description applies to you and me, for we too are those who have been called to follow, and are loved by God (Jude 1).

Why, then, do so many people find it difficult to receive such a truth? For some, the reason lies in the fact that they find it hard to feel the love of God. They believe it in their minds, but can't feel it in their hearts. Such a person was Dr David Benner, an American psychologist. He has shared how, for many years, he substituted ideas about God for a direct experience of him. His faith was more about intellectual assent than about emotional reliance or trust. During his 30s he became deeply dissatisfied with his limited experience of God and the fact that he didn't know God's love on a deep, persistent and personal basis. His hunger led him to read many of the classics of Christian spirituality and to discover contemplative prayer. Gradually he began to meet God not just in his head but in his heart. Now he writes, 'The fact that I am deeply loved by God is increasingly the core of my identity, what I know about myself with most confidence. Such a conviction is, I am convinced, the foundation of any significant Christian spiritual growth.'[34]

For other people, the issue is more about not being able to receive love, and this is often due to either a deep sense of being unlovable or a feeling of not deserving such love. When we have been damaged emotionally, and have perhaps been hurt or rejected by others, it is easy to import our feelings of mistrust into our relationship with God. This makes it difficult for us to hear the voice of love. It seems too good to be true. It may apply to others, but such a blessing could never be for us personally.

How can we start to receive God's love? It begins, I think, with the understanding that it is primarily a question of God's love for me, not my love for him. John said that we love because God first loved us (1 John 4:19). The prior love of God must be our starting point. My love is only ever in response to his love for me. I must fix my gaze upon him and think deeply about the unconditional nature of his love. Why does he love me? Because I am good enough? No! Because I deserve it? No! He loves me because it is his nature to love.

As we have been reminded already, God is love. Love is the essence of who he is. I can no more stop God loving me than I can prevent the sun from shining on me—and God's sun shines on the just and the unjust alike! (Matthew 5:45). Love is not merely an attribute of God or an emotion that comes and goes according to my behaviour. It is his essence. He loves me simply because he is love. He cannot help it. However unworthy I may feel, and however undeserving I may be, the fact remains that I am the object of divine love. I may as well get used to the fact.

This is where the discipline of receiving love comes into play. I must agree with God that I am indeed his beloved child, no matter how I feel about myself. The answer is in him, not in me. He has said that I am his beloved child, and I must agree with him and say so with my lips. Meditating upon these truths can help enormously. So can contemplative prayer, for in the stillness it is often easier to hear the whisper of love. Healing prayer may help, as will talking openly and honestly about what is going on inside us. Perfect love casts out fear (1 John 4:18). Knowing that God accepts me as I am can give me the confidence to face the worst about myself, knowing that I am loved for who I am. Nothing is hidden from God. He has seen the worst of me, and he loves me just the same. If I dare to step into the ocean of his love, I will find it a healing and liberating experience.

The invitation to make our home in the love of God is not one to be rejected. The key to loving others is knowing myself to be loved. The house of love is the place of transformation, and it is where I belong. A growing awareness that we are deeply loved by God releases us to be able to love God as well as other people. Having received love, we are free to give love. This is the heart of all fruitful living. The more we abide, the more abundant will be the harvest of our lives.

✣

The father
Holds his new-born baby in his arms
And sings the love song
Of his heart.
Protective, proud,
Eyes bright with tears
For the life about to start.

In weakness
Helplessly the baby lies,
Love enfolded
New life just begun.
Love guaranteed
Because he is his father's son.

I do not
Have to strive to gain my Father's love,
Deserve or merit,
Work to please.
From His full heart
He sings to me,
And loves me
Just because I'm His.

BARBARA PARSONS

15

THE DISCIPLINE
OF OBEDIENCE

If you obey my commands, you will remain in my love, just as I have obeyed my Father's commands and remain in his love (v. 10).

The invitation from Jesus to live within the circle of love is at the same time a call to live within the realm of surrender to the Father's will. In kingdom terms, to love is to obey. If we claim to know God, the proof will be in the reality of our obedience to his commands. Our responsive love for God is expressed in doing his will. As John says elsewhere, 'This is love for God: to obey his commands' (1 John 5:3).

It is a law of the spiritual life that obedience leads to abiding. Rees Howells was a Welshman with an amazing ministry of intercession. The story of his life, and the dramatic answers to prayer that characterized his ministry, is told in the book *Intercessor* by Norman Grubb.[35] In his preparation for prayer, Rees Howells always sought what he called the 'place of abiding'. I think by this he meant the awareness of his position 'in Christ' and the fact of Christ living in him. This position was maintained by a careful obedience to the Holy Spirit. The key to his spiritual authority seems to have rested in his willingness to obey every prompting of the Holy Spirit, no matter how small.

Jesus himself lived in the discipline of obedience. His only desire was to please the Father. David speaks prophetically of him, placing these words in his mouth: 'Then I said, "Here I am, I have come— it is written about me in the scroll. I desire to do your will, O my

God; your law is within my heart"' (Psalm 40:7–8; Hebrews 10:7). This attitude characterized his life on earth. He came into the world with a mission from the Father. He had a purpose, a work to complete, and it summed up his whole life. Even as a child he was aware that he must be 'about his Father's business' (Luke 2:49, KJV). This was what motivated and energized him. 'My food,' he said, 'is to do the will of him who sent me and to finish his work' (John 4:34). And again, 'For I have come down from heaven not to do my will but to do the will of him who sent me' (John 6:38).

The heart of Jesus' mission was to lay down his life on the cross. This was the ultimate expression of the obedience that epitomized his life (Romans 5:19). No matter what the cost, he was determined to choose the Father's will ahead of his own (Matthew 26:39). His sacrifice at Calvary was made freely and willingly out of love for the Father. 'The reason my Father loves me is that I lay down my life—only to take it up again. No one takes it from me, but I lay it down of my own accord. I have authority to lay it down and authority to take it up again. This command I received from my Father' (John 10:17–18). This was the work he was determined to complete (John 17:4), and the reason he cried out, 'It is finished!' as he died (John 19:30). He had been obedient even to the point of death (Philippians 2:8).

In this, as in everything else, Jesus is the pattern for us. His life of complete surrender to the Father's will is the model for our own glad surrender. 'Christian spirituality,' notes David Benner, 'is following Christ in this self-abandonment. It is following his example of willing surrender.'[36]

I am conscious that, for some, this idea of surrender to the will of God is a difficult, even painful one. For those who have found themselves taken advantage of, or maybe even abused by religious leaders, this is a sensitive area. Having given ourselves completely once, and been let down, we do not easily want to offer ourselves again. I am aware, too, that in calling for 'commitment' some leaders inadvertently place others under religious bondage and legalism. All of these pitfalls we wish to avoid.

The surrender we are speaking of here is a surrender to love, not to authority or power. It is yielding ourselves to a God who loves us magnificently, and who only desires to do us good. Once we have got hold of this, we dare to offer ourselves up to him, for we realize that his will really is good, pleasing and perfect (Romans 12:2). It is something to be embraced, not avoided.

As a Christian psychologist and spiritual director, David Benner has written very wisely on this whole understanding of surrender to love:

Christian surrender is saying Yes to God's Yes! to me. It begins as I experience his wildly enthusiastic, recklessly loving affirmation of me. It grows out of soaking myself in this love so thoroughly that love for God springs up in response. Surrender to his love is the work of his Spirit, making his love ours and his nature ours. This is the core of Christian spiritual transformation.[37]

Thus the discipline of receiving love must come before the discipline of obedience. The former must be the grounds of the latter, for what God looks for is loving obedience, an obedience of the heart, and not mere compliance (Romans 6:17). Christian obedience should always be based on our surrender to the one who has lavished his love upon us, not just the keeping of rules and regulations or religious duty. It is this that distinguishes legalistic obedience ('I ought to... must... should... have to...') from a grace-based obedience ('I want to...'). It is this that puts the word 'glad' into the expression 'glad surrender'. Once we have allowed God to win our hearts with his love, obedience to his will follows naturally and easily. It becomes the desire of our hearts.

Having cleared our minds of these difficulties, we are now free to hear in these verses the call of Jesus to fruitful living. Just as he came into this world on a mission from the Father, so he sends us out into the world to bear fruit for him. As we abide in his love, we shall inevitably hear the whisper of his command to 'go'. Knowing ourselves loved so deeply, we are ready to respond, whatever it may mean for us.

Jesus summed up all the commandments of the Old Testament into just two: love God and love your neighbour (Matthew 22:36–40). He then added a third: love one another (John 13:34–35), which means that the Christian life becomes simply a matter of love. As we receive love from God, we share it with one another and then release it into the world around us. It is not that we are following a moral code, or a list of dos and don'ts; we are allowing the love of God within us to flow out from us. That is why his commandments are not burdensome, for he is actually creating within us the desire to please him, and giving us all that we need in order to do what he asks of us (1 John 5:3). As followers of Jesus, these are the commandments and the lifestyle to which we are committed.

It seems that in what Jesus is saying here we have actually a foretaste of the great commission, which he would later give to the disciples in more detail, and which has been the mandate for much of the church's activity in evangelism and mission (Matthew 28:18–20). His whispered 'Go' has meant, for many, a call to leave their comfortable surroundings and move into cross-cultural ministry. For others, it has meant giving up job and career in order to serve the church more fully. People have been sent by him into education, the health services, social work, business and industry, politics and entertainment… each with a clear call to bear fruit in their own particular context. They go with a realization that 'commission' implies co-mission—a sharing with God in what he is doing in the world around.

As well as these general callings that require obedience, there are the more personal commands that come to us individually. Often described as 'promptings' of the Spirit, they are integral to our own abiding in Christ. We may have a feeling to pray for someone or a burden to speak with a particular person about the good news of the gospel. It could be an internal nudge to give someone a call, or the desire to help someone out practically. It might even be an insight that something needs to change in our own behaviour. These impressions can come in any number of ways, and as we begin to discern the voice of God more clearly we are able to recognize such moments more easily. It is important that we obey these inner promptings. They are the expression of a living relationship with a God who speaks, and are a reminder that his life is at work within us.

When I think of surrender and obedience, a picture comes into my mind. It is of two ice skaters, perhaps like the famous British pair of Jane Torvill and Christopher Dean. As we watch them skate over the ice, we see that they are in harmony, moving to the rhythm of the music. The two are in perfect union and they move as one. They have learned to anticipate one another, to respond to one another, to sense what the other is doing. Where he leads, she willingly follows. It is a wonderful picture of the oneness that can exist between Christ and the believer. As we learn to surrender ourselves to his lead, and follow gladly in his steps, we can become one with him in his plans and purposes for the world.

Obedience is the channel that allows the life of God to flow through us and bear fruit. Disobedience, on the other hand, restricts the flow of life and leaves us barren and unfruitful. As Andrew Murray says, 'Each new surrender to keep His commandments, each new sacrifice in keeping them, leads to a deeper union with the will, the spirit, and the love of the Saviour.'[38] This is the path of obedience that we are called to walk. The deeper union is its reward and blessing.

✢

As the music began
He held her,
Embraced her.
He led and she followed his leading,
Gliding,
Swaying
Dancing, lightfooted and graceful:
Two people moving as one;
Two people,
Hearing the same song.

And this is obedience:
Moving to His music,
His leading: my following,
Giving me a grace I do not possess,
A beauty that is not my own,
A love song
Sung for me alone.

BARBARA PARSONS

16

THE DISCIPLINE OF INTIMACY

Greater love has no one than this, that he lay down his life for his friends. You are my friends if you do what I command. I no longer call you servants, because a servant does not know his master's business. Instead, I have called you friends, for everything that I learned from my Father I have made known to you (vv. 13–15).

Just across the road from where I live is the village war memorial. It is a stone cross inscribed with the names of all those from the village who died in the two World Wars. Many of the names are familiar to me as their families still live here. Written at the foot of the cross are the words from John 15:13: 'Greater love has no one than this, that he lay down his life for his friends.'

Each year on Remembrance Sunday a simple ceremony reminds us of the bravery and sacrifice of these men. Human love causes people to perform many heroic acts, not just in time of war but also in times of crisis or danger. It is humbling to consider the lengths to which people will go in self-sacrifice for those whom they love. It is one of the brighter aspects of human nature.

The death of Jesus on the cross was just such an act of love, but it was much more than that. His death was more than a noble sacrifice or heroic martyrdom for those he loved. He actually died for those who were his enemies, for those who had turned their backs on God and were living in their own rebellious ways. Paul explains it like this: 'Very rarely will anyone die for a righteous man, though for a good man someone might possibly dare to die. But God demonstrates his own love for us in this: While we were sinners, Christ died for us' (Romans 5:7–8).

All of us, because of our personal sinfulness, find ourselves identified in this group for whom Christ died. The reason he died was to bring us back to God, so that we could once again enjoy friendship and intimacy with him. In the garden of Eden, Adam and Eve had originally shared such fellowship with God, but sin spoilt that relationship and broke the bond between them. Those of us born subsequently, and 'in Adam', are actually born estranged from God—his enemies, not friends. The cross, however, makes it possible for us to be reconciled to him and for the friendship to be restored. Reconciliation is the process by which enemies are made friends again, and this is one of the outstanding results of Christ's death. 'All this is from God,' says Paul, 'who reconciled us to himself through Christ and gave us the ministry of reconciliation: that God was reconciling the world to himself in Christ, not counting men's sins against them' (2 Corinthians 5:18–19).

Anticipating the work of the cross, Jesus now invites his disciples into an altogether different kind of relationship with himself. No longer are they to think of themselves as servants, whose task is busily to do their master's bidding. They are to see themselves as his friends, those invited into the inner circle of his companionship, who share his confidence. This change perhaps represents the difference between the old covenant and the new. Formerly, the intimate knowledge of God and his ways was limited to a few privileged individuals. Under the new covenant, everyone can know God personally and deeply, whatever their standing or background in life (Hebrews 8:10–12).

Of course the servant metaphor is an important one throughout the scriptures, and we are called to involve ourselves in the work of the kingdom. It is not the only picture, however, and neither is it the most foundational. The metaphor of friendship is even more basic, for our service for God is meant to flow out of a relationship of closeness and intimacy. It is important that we see ourselves primarily as 'friends', otherwise we may miss out on the level of intimacy that God has called us to. He desires our fellowship first and foremost, and wants us to serve him out of relationship, not just out of obligation or duty.

I recently attended my school reunion. It was the first time that most of us had met up since our graduation in 1968. It was interesting to note that some people had changed very little and were still easily recognizable, while others (like me!) had changed considerably. The conversation flowed freely all evening, the talk loud and animated as people reconnected with each other. I wondered why, having once been such good friends, we had drifted apart. I suppose it is easy, if you move to another part of the country, follow a different career path and develop new interests, to leave old friends behind, even though you promise to keep in touch. One thing I noticed, however, was that with the most genuine friendships the 'spark' was still there, and it was relatively easy to reconnect.

The discipline of intimacy is primarily about seeing ourselves as 'friends' of God and developing the kind of intimacy that characterizes a good friendship. Friends spend time together, and, as we have already seen, giving quality time to our walk with God is a fundamental aspect of abiding in Christ. In the busyness of life it is easy to drift away from God, despite our own good intentions to stay close to him. We need to be willing to 'waste' time simply being in his presence, with no agenda other than to be together. We discipline ourselves to meet with God on a regular basis, and avoid the danger of being so busy doing things for God that we have no time to be with him.

With friends, we do not need many words. We are happy to enjoy a companionable silence. There seems to be a link between a growing intimacy with God and silent (or contemplative) prayer. John Dalrymple, a Scottish priest, noted how progress in intimacy becomes a progress towards silence. This happens in human friendship, and the friendship of prayer follows a similar pattern. He wrote:

Intimacy in prayer comes when we find we can remain in communion with God without any particular desire to move on to some business with him. We are content just to stay with God, conscious that he loves us, trying to respond with our own love. We dwell with God, and he with us. It is difficult to put into words what happens when prayer simplifies like this.[39]

Something that undoubtedly happens at such moments is that communication takes place at a very deep level. We become responsive and receptive to the other. Indeed, we might say that 'communion' is what happens when two hearts connect without having to say much. Not only do we talk, but we also listen. These are the moments of revelation when Jesus communicates his heart to us, when he reveals to us the Father's plans and purposes. We may not know everything, but we begin to know something. The servant generally has no sense of this connection, but the friend is drawn into the mind and will of the master. He operates from a place of understanding, of knowing what is on the master's heart.

Intimacy with God does not deflect us from involvement in a needy world, but rather directs our efforts to make us efficient and effective in what we do. The danger of the servant mentality is that, in the desire to be doing something (anything), we can be like the fishermen disciples: we toil all night and catch nothing. Good ideas are not necessarily God's ideas, and activity is not an end in itself. The friend, on the other hand, listens for the word of command ('Throw your net on the right side of the boat'), and responds in obedience, which proves to be fruitful, for it is both God-originated and God-directed (see John 21:1–9). The discipline of intimacy is important if our involvement in the master's business is to be productive. It enables us to develop a listening heart.

The friendship metaphor carries with it an implicit emphasis on devotion. Jesus is the friend of sinners (Matthew 11:19). He is the friend who loves at all times, the one who sticks closer than a brother (Proverbs 17:17; 18:24). Supremely, he is the one who lays down his life for his friends. To be called into friendship and fellowship with such a person is indeed a privilege. His friendship kindles a response of passionate devotion in those who know him, which provides the energy and motivation for service.

Job could speak of the days when God's intimate friendship blessed his house (Job 29:4). The hymn writer Samuel Crossman captured this feeling so well in his beautiful hymn 'My song is love unknown'. First he saw the cross and the debt he owed: 'But O my friend, my friend indeed, who at my need his life did spend.' Then he made his response and brought his worship: 'This is my friend, in whose sweet praise I all my days could gladly spend.'

The discovery that we can be friends with God through Jesus transforms our whole approach to Christian living. It lifts us out of the realm of drudgery and duty and places us into the realm of privilege and passion. It inspires us to abide in Christ and to make his presence our dwelling place. It releases us to know God more deeply and to serve him more fruitfully.

✣

God walked with Adam
In the cool of the day,
Intimate moments,
Strolling together:
Laughing,
Sharing,
Friends

But all this was lost
When Adam left Eden
His loss and God's loss:
Soul mates no longer
Lonely,
Grieving
Bereft

And then came the Cross,
Restoring, redeeming
Our broken friendship,
God's arms spread in welcome,
Holding me close,
Back home.

So why is it now,
Reconciled, forgiven
At such great cost,
I don't walk
With my Father
In the cool
Of the day.

BARBARA PARSONS

QUESTIONS FOR REFLECTION

For individuals

1. How does the discipline of dependency express itself? What part does prayer currently play in your life? Does it show your need of God or your tendency to depend on yourself?
2. How do the scriptures help us to abide? In what ways do you allow the word of God to dwell in you?
3. Why is receiving love considered to be a discipline? Are you secure in your identity as a beloved child or do you find it difficult to receive love? What can you do to receive more of God's love?
4. Are you fully surrendered to God? What examples could you give of responding to his call to 'Go', or to the more personal promptings that require obedience? How will you deal with any outstanding issues of obedience?
5. Which metaphor do you tend to live by—that of the servant or that of the friend? How would it affect your relationship to God if you were more aware of being his friend?

For groups

1. Which two groups of people are most prone to depend on their natural strength? How does prayer express our dependency on God? What can we learn from Jesus?
2. In what five ways can we soak ourselves in the scriptures? How will this help us to abide in Christ and be more fruitful?
3. Why is it important to discover our identity as God's beloved children? Why do some people find this difficult? What can help us to receive God's love?
4. How does the idea of obedience as surrender to love help us? How have you been challenged to obey God recently? What is your motivation for obedience?

5. What does the Christian life look like when seen through (a) the servant metaphor, and (b) the friendship metaphor? How can you develop intimacy with God?

THE HARVEST OF THE VINE:
NATURAL OUTCOMES

17

ANSWERED PRAYER

If you remain in me and my words remain in you, ask whatever you wish, and it will be given you (v. 7)… Then the Father will give you whatever you ask in my name (v. 16).

We now begin to consider the outcomes of abiding in Christ. We said earlier that by fruit we mean 'any outward expression of the life of God within', and have noted that it is God's will that our lives should bear much fruit. This is how we glorify him and prove the reality of our own discipleship.

It has often been pointed out that a progression in fruit-bearing can be seen in these verses. The process of cleansing takes us from bearing no fruit to bearing some fruit. Pruning takes us from bearing some fruit to bearing more fruit. It is when we abide fully in Christ, however, that we begin to bear much fruit. This is the abundant harvest that the vine dresser longs for, and for which he is prepared to work so hard.

Prayer is not only one of the key elements in abiding; it is also one of the outcomes, an expression of the life of God within us. Having learned the *big* lesson that apart from Christ we can do nothing, prayer becomes a natural and vital expression of our dependency on God. By spending time in the presence of Jesus, we have a greater desire to pray and a clearer sense of what we should be asking for. Thus our prayer becomes more effective. Answered prayer is part of the harvest of the abiding life.

For most of us, however, prayer remains a mystery. It often feels like playing a game of darts. We take careful aim and shoot at the bull's-eye. Sometimes we hit; sometimes we miss. So it is with our prayers. Sometimes we pray, and the answer is there immediately—a hit! Another time we pray and nothing seems to happen—a miss! Most of the time we do not understand either why our prayers are heard or why at other times it seems that they are not.

I do not think that, this side of heaven, we will ever finally reduce prayer to a working formula that is successful every time. Indeed, unanswered prayer is one of the factors that keep us dependent upon God, and our weakness in this area gives us more room to allow the Holy Spirit to pray through us (Romans 8:26). However, Jesus teaches clearly here that we can definitely receive answers to our prayers, and that praying can make a significant difference to what happens. We should not lose heart if we cannot always work it out.

What, then, is the key to effective prayer? When we look at the wider sweep of biblical teaching on prayer, the touchstone seems to be that prayer is the means by which God's will is brought to pass on the earth. Thus, in the model prayer that Jesus taught us, the main petition is, 'Your kingdom come, your will be done on earth as it is in heaven' (Matthew 6:10). The big mistake we often make in prayer is to think of it as a way of getting God to do what we want to happen. This turns prayer upside down. If we approach it from this perspective, it will never work, for it is operating out of a wrong basic assumption. This is why James says, 'When you ask, you do not receive, because you ask with wrong motives, that you may spend what you get on your pleasures' (James 4:3). Wrong motivation is not just asking for self-centred benefits. It is asking for anything that is out of line with the good and perfect will of God, however well-meaning our prayers may be.

The clearest expression of this foundational prayer principle occurs in John's first letter: 'This is the confidence we have in approaching God: that if we ask anything *according to his will*, he hears us. And if we know that he hears us—whatever we ask—we know that we have what we asked of him' (1 John 5:14–15, my italics). We can have authority in prayer and be confident of the outcome, when we have learned to pray according to God's will.

What needs to happen if we are to pray effectively is that our hearts must be changed drastically, from a focus on me and my will to a focus on God and his will. This is a massive shift in perspective, and writer John Dalrymple likens it to a Copernican revolution. At first we see ourselves as the centre of the world, and God is on the circumference, ready to do our bidding. Then the real revolution takes place. We realize that God is actually at the centre of the universe. It is we who are on the circumference, and we exist to do his bidding.

We pass from thinking of God as part of our life to the realization that we are part of his life. There is a shift in the centre of gravity... Instead of granting God a place in my life, the realization dawns that he is Creator and he has granted a place to me in his life.[40]

This is the change that God is working towards as we abide in him and allow his word to abide in us. First it cleanses us of our sin, and then it prunes us of our selfishness. Then, as we allow it to find a place in our hearts, it begins to alter our basic disposition and orientation so that we begin to want what God wants. This inner transformation is the result of abiding in Christ, and it prepares us for the responsibility of praying with authority.

The word of God is the will of God, and the more I am at home within it, the more I will have the mind of Christ. As I soak up the teaching of scripture, my mind is renewed and my thoughts are brought into line with God's thoughts. In the place of intimacy and abiding, a harmony is forged between God's will and my own will. I begin to understand his plans and share his purposes. It brings me to the point where I can say, as one of my friends often does, 'If God's happy, then I'm happy.'

Having become one with God in his will and purpose, we can then be entrusted with the authority of prayer, for here we are given a blank cheque, as it were, to ask God whatever we wish. Since we have taken our delight in the Lord, he can confidently give us the desires of our hearts (Psalm 37:4), because our will has become one with his. Further, knowing that we share his concerns, he can confidently send us into the world 'in his name' because he knows that we will faithfully represent him. As we obey his command to 'go', anything we need to accomplish his purpose is now at our disposal. No obstacle can stand in our way as we seek to glorify him in our lives. The scene is set for some dramatic answers to our prayers.

Elijah is a character in the Bible with whom we associate dramatic answers to prayer, and yet he is presented to us as an ordinary man—indeed, a man of 'like passions' with us (James 5:17, KJV), human like the rest of us. He prayed that it would not rain, and there was a drought for three and a half years. Again he prayed, and the rain came once more. His secret? He stood in the presence of God (1 Kings 17:1, KJV). He maintained a place of intimacy with God, and had discerned the mind of God for the perilous times in which he lived. This gave him his confidence in prayer. His story assures us that 'the prayer of a person living right with God is something powerful to be reckoned with' (James 5:16, *THE MESSAGE*).

Many books have been written about answered prayer. The history of the Church is full of testimony to the fact that God can, and does, answer prayer, and that the prayers of his people have had a major impact in determining the outcome of events. Some of these answered prayers are on a macro scale—events that have affected world history and shaped the destiny of whole nations. Others are on a micro scale, reflecting the personal response of a loving God to our individual needs. I would like to share just two examples.

The first concerns a slightly eccentric lady who was a member of our church and had a great belief in the power of prayer. She also had a burden for the communist world in the days of the Cold War. Twice she visited Albania as a 'tourist', and, along with others, visited some of the key cities to pray for the overthrow of that stifling regime. Whenever we had a prayer meeting, Joyce would ask that we pray for Albania. I have to say to my shame that I thought it was another of her 'eccentricities' and that nothing would change the powerful grip of communism on that atheistic land. We humoured her, but Joyce continued to believe that God would do something special.

Imagine our surprise when communism fell and Albania opened up to the gospel. Joyce was able to visit a third time, to freely and openly share the gospel with the people of the country that God had laid on her heart. 'Ask whatever you will,' Jesus said. Understanding the heart of God more clearly than the rest of us, Joyce chose to ask that Albania would become a free country, and that the gospel would take root there. God heard her prayer (and that of many others) and granted her bold request.

The second story concerns a group of children who were attending an Alpha course held especially for them during the school holidays. They were very enthusiastic in the games and Bible study that were part of the weekly programme. After one session they were invited to share any requests for prayer. One girl told how her pet rabbit had been missing for nearly two weeks. She was sure it was lost for ever, but could they pray and ask God to bring it back? The group leader was a little hesitant, but seeing the faith of the children, she agreed that they should pray.

Not long after they finished praying, while they were tidying up, there was a knock on the door. It was two boys from the neighbourhood. 'Missus,' they said in a broad Yorkshire accent to the lady of the house. 'We've found a rabbit and we're going round to ask who it belongs to.' Imagine the delight of the children when they saw it and identified it as the missing rabbit. From that day on it was known as 'the Alpha rabbit', a very powerful reminder to the children of the willingness of God to answer prayer.

When we are abiding in Christ and allowing his word to abide in us, we have in prayer a mighty weapon at our disposal. Nothing need stand in our way as we seek to do God's will and bring his kingdom to pass in our communities. We are connected to a living God, an all-powerful and loving God. Nothing is too difficult for him, and nothing is too small for his attention. We can move forward with confidence and see every obstacle and hindrance removed, and all our needs supplied as we give ourselves to his purpose.

The only reason we do not have is because we do not ask (James 4:2). When we do ask, heaven waits to grant our requests.

❖

Prayer: God's invitation to stand beside him in his will

Prayer is heaven's open door
Bold access to Your Throne;
My heart at ease, delighted
In my heart's heavenly home.

Prayer is my deep joy shared,
It is my spirit's groan,
It is 'Your will be done, not mine'
It is Your will
Become my own.

BARBARA PARSONS

18

SUPERNATURAL JOY

I have told you this so that my joy may be in you and that your joy may be complete (v. 11).

When I am in the dentist's waiting room (which in my case is often), I invariably search for a copy of the *Reader's Digest*. Having found some out-of-date edition, I then turn to the section called 'Laughter: the best medicine' and have a little chuckle to myself. I have found this a tried-and-tested formula for reducing the stress of anticipated pain!

I think we all recognize that laughter is good for us. The book of Proverbs saw this long ago, reminding us that a cheerful heart is good medicine (17:22). The current thinking in health and healing is that laughter and joyfulness increase the efficiency of the immune system and speed up the healing process both physically and psychologically.

Unfortunately, Christianity is not always associated with laughter or happiness. All too often it is perceived as solemn, serious and sombre. What a travesty this is, especially when we consider the truth of this verse—that Jesus came to share his joy with us as one of the fruits of abiding in him. Joyless Christianity is a contradiction in terms, for those who have the divine life welling up within them are inevitably bursting with joy.

The God of the Bible is a happy God. He is one who laughs, if perhaps a little ironically, at the machinations of the world's rulers (Psalm 2:4) and who delights to see his people have a good time. In his presence there is fullness of joy (Psalm 16:11; Acts 2:28). The three annual festivals of the Old Testament were an opportunity for the people to celebrate and let their hair down, to discover that the joy of the Lord was their strength (Nehemiah 8:10). At the feast of Tabernacles, for example, they were told, 'Be joyful at your Feast… For seven days celebrate the Feast to the Lord your God… For the Lord your God will bless you in all your harvest and in all the work of your hands, and your joy will be complete' (Deuteronomy 16:14–15). Worship is meant to be a happy experience when God's people come before the Lord, joyful and glad in heart, with singing and music and dancing, to celebrate his goodness (for example, Psalm 92:1–4; 95:1–2; 98:4–6; 100:1–2).

Not surprisingly, Jesus portrays the Father as one who is prodigal (lavishly wasteful) in his love and kindness. In the story of the two sons (Luke 15:11–32), the focus of attention is actually on the grace and generosity of the father, who kills the fatted calf and throws a party to celebrate when his wandering son returns. Music and dancing are the sounds of the father's house—not the wildness of hedonism, but the unrestrained joy of grace. 'We had to celebrate and be glad,' he says to the sulking elder brother, 'because this brother of yours was dead and is alive again; he was lost and is found' (Luke 15:32). Heaven knows how to rejoice!

Although Jesus is often described as the man of sorrows (Isaiah 53:3), he is equally the man of joy. He was anointed with the oil of gladness (Psalm 45:7; Hebrews 1:9), which suggests that he had a cheerful disposition, and knew how to laugh and have fun. In *The Gospel Road*, a film made by Johnny Cash in the 1970s, I love the scene where Jesus and the disciples are walking along the road as they travel from town to town. They are behaving like any other group of men would—laughing and joking, pushing and shoving each other playfully, having a good time as they hang out together. And Jesus is the centre of the fun!

There were moments in his earthly life when he was clearly and visibly filled with joy (Luke 10:21). His teaching was sprinkled with humour, and he often spoke with a twinkle in his eye. From riddles to amusing parables, from plays on words to subtle irony, from absurd situations to memorable catch-phrases, he communicated in ways that made people laugh and see the truth about themselves and God.[41] The disciples knew he was good to be with and easy to be around. They enjoyed his company, and so did others, for he was as relaxed at Simon's party (Luke 7:36) as he was in the synagogue.

When it came to the most serious moment of all in his life, he faced the cross in the light of 'the joy set before him' (Hebrews 12:2). Having dealt with sin and opened the way for us to return to God, he is now seated at the Father's right hand and has received the full measure of that joy which was his inspiration on earth. The risen, ascended, victorious Lord is indeed a man of joy who desires now to share his joy with us. He longs that our patchy, earthbound joy may be completed with his heavenly, supernatural joy, so that we may experience the full measure of his joy within us (John 17:13). This is part of the exchanged life, the fruit of his life remaining in us.

No wonder, then, that joy is part of the fruit of the Spirit, a key evidence of salvation and a sign that the kingdom of God has come. We watch the first disciples and see that even in the midst of trial and persecution they were filled with great joy (Acts 8:8; 13:52). We see individuals coming to faith and finding themselves over-whelmed with an inexpressible and glorious joy, which, according to Peter, is the goal or end-product of faith (Acts 16:34; 1 Peter 1:8–9). We see them gathering together in joyful assembly as they celebrate together the goodness of God (Colossians 3:16; Ephesians 5:19–20). 'Joy in the city' aptly summarizes the result of New Testament evangelism. Righteousness, peace and joy mark out the kingdom (Romans 14:17).

Such joy is supernatural. It is communicated to us through the Holy Spirit, and is the product of the life of Jesus within us. It is supernatural firstly because it transcends human personality or temperament. Some people are by nature optimistic, while others are pessimistic. For some the glass is always half-full; for others it is half-empty. Some see opportunities, others only problems. The exciting thing about the joy of Jesus is that it can lighten up even the gloomiest of personalities. If we are willing, he can take the garments of our heaviness and exchange them for his own garments of praise. He can be glad within us, and make us joyful when we might otherwise be serious and intense. The more we dwell in his presence, the more we begin to share his positive disposition. Even those who are naturally sunnier in outlook can discover a deeper joy within them and find that they no longer need to depend on the power of their human personality alone.

This joy is supernatural secondly because it transcends circumstances and situations. The basic difference between happiness and joy is that happiness is dependent on external happenings (things going well), whereas joy is a more deep-seated and constant sense of well-being that is based on an awareness of God's unchanging and protecting love. Happiness tends to come and go; joy is more consistent and abiding. If we want to, even in the most difficult of times we can receive the joy of Jesus into our lives. It is a choice we make—either to be dominated by circumstances and become depressed and downhearted, or to depend on Jesus and his life within us and remain faith-filled and optimistic. I am not thinking here of an inappropriate joy. There is a time to laugh and a time to weep; a time to dance and a time to mourn (Ecclesiastes 3:4). What I am saying is that the general tenor of our lives can be more towards joy than sadness.

The letter to the Philippians is often called 'the epistle of joy' because it vibrates with hope and confidence, yet it was written while Paul was imprisoned and his own situation very bleak. Rather than be despondent, though, he chose to become aware of the working of God within him (Philippians 1:6; 2:13) and to rejoice in his circumstances (1:18). This meant more than just pulling himself together or putting on a brave face. It was possible because of his intimacy with Jesus, which extended to sharing in the fellowship of his sufferings (3:7–11). It came as a result of his union with Christ and his conscious choice to abide in his presence and depend on his life. He urges us to do the same: 'Rejoice in the Lord always. I will say it again: Rejoice!' (4:4). It is gloriously possible to rise above both our circumstances and our temperaments.

Joyfulness is such an attractive quality. Imagine the attractiveness of a community that is full of joy! This is what the church is called to be, and it is possible when, as individuals and corporately, we learn to abide in Christ. Sadly, many have failed to tap into the joy of Jesus, often because they have never been taught how to deepen their walk with him. They have never discovered what singer and broadcaster Sheila Walsh calls 'the incredible lightness of grace'. Reflecting on her own story, with its failure and disappointments and her subsequent discovery of the unconditional love of God, she says:

When you have faced the worst there is to know about yourself and experienced the gift of grace, life is new and wonderful... The joy that springs out of grace is so different from mere happiness... Grace embraced all that was good and true and all that was bad and faithless about me. Grace is love with its eyes wide open.[42]

The church has often failed to reflect the joyfulness of its head—Jesus himself. Church life can become very serious and intense, full of politics and in-fighting, a dreadful advertisement for the good news that Jesus came to bring. We become more concerned for doctrinal accuracy and scrupulous behaviour than for the new life that is ours in Christ. No wonder we have difficulty in communicating our message when we are so lacking in joy. It is vital that we rediscover the joy of Jesus, lighten up a little, and get in touch again with the true source of our life.

Only an authentic, Christ-dependent church can hope to survive or meet the challenges of a postmodern and post-Christian society. Only joy-filled communities will attract and win a sceptical and questioning generation. There is no limit or hesitation on the part of Jesus. He longs to share his abundant life with us. For our part, we must be willing to see our need and to reconnect with him in the place of abiding.

✣

The world's joy
Is like a butterfly:
Flitting and fluttering
Against the window of life
Trying to escape.

To hold it is to bruise it
So its visit is brief,
Delighting for a moment,
Then winging its ragged flight
Into the distance.

The Spirit's joy
Is not a fragile, fleeting thing:
It is a gushing fountain,
Living, bursting from the soul,
Unquenchable, Unstoppable,
Immeasurable.

So why do we, His people,
Turn from dancing in the fountain
To the cracked well of legalism,
Criticism and intolerance,
Letting joy die
In the mire of our politics?
No wonder the world prefers a glimpsed butterfly.

Let's return to the fountain,
Plunging in,
For joy is boundless
When we are lost in Him.

BARBARA PARSONS

19

LOVING COMMUNITY

My command is this: Love each other as I have loved you (v. 12)…
This is my command: Love each other (v. 17).

Implicit in the words of Jesus in John 15 is his intention to establish a community among his followers. Overall, he spoke surprisingly little about the church, but in this command to love one another we can see that one of the fruits of his own life would be the formation of a community of people dedicated to doing his will.

We have already noted that the picture of the vine and its branches is essentially plural in its application. Although we have looked at abiding in Christ as it applies to us as individuals, one of the dangers of an emphasis on intimacy is that it becomes too intensely personal. To find its most mature expression, intimacy with God has to be played out in the context of community, not in splendid isolation but in relationship with others. It is about 'us' and not just 'me'.

The mark of this new community will be love—not a sentimental, romantic notion, but a love that has practical expression in the ups and downs of life together. Jesus calls us to love one another in the same way that he has loved us. If we abide in him, his love will be reproduced within us, enabling us to love those around us. 'Love is the acid test of Christian spirituality,' notes David Benner. 'If Christian conversion is authentic, we are in a process of becoming more loving. If we are not becoming more loving, something is seriously wrong.'[43]

This new community is not to be centred on rules and regulations, but on the outward expression of the life of God within us. Since God is love, the presence of his life within us begins to transform us into loving people, and this love is the fulfilling of the law. 'Let no debt remain outstanding,' says Paul, 'except the continuing debt to love one another, for he who loves his fellow man has fulfilled the law. The commandments, "Do not commit adultery," "Do not murder," "Do not steal," "Do not covet," and whatever other commandment there may be, are summed up in this one rule: "Love your neighbour as yourself." Love does no harm to its neighbour. Therefore love is the fulfilment of the law' (Romans 13:8–10).

This 'one rule' is what James calls the 'royal law', where we choose to love our neighbour as ourselves (James 2:8). It is the outworking of the new commandment that Jesus gave his followers, the identifying mark of true disciples (John 13:34–35). It is the brotherly love that characterized the first Christian communities, which Peter says flows from the heart of those who have experienced the new birth (1 Peter 1:22; 2:17; 3:8; 4:8). It is the self-giving love that, according to the beloved disciple, enables us to put the needs of others before our own, and to lay down our lives for them (1 John 3:16–17).

The failure of many Christian churches to be communities of love does not mean that this is an impossible ideal. The love we are speaking about is supernatural in its origin. However loving we may be in ourselves, human love will never be sufficient. We will need to be filled with God's own love so that it can overflow from us. Only as we abide in Christ can we know ourselves to be loved, and thus have a surplus of love to impart to others. It is not about trying harder to love, but about abiding more closely. Further, it will require us to be willing to die to ourselves and experience the cross at work in our own lives. We will have to step outside the boundaries of self-interest and self-absorption if the loving life of God is to be released from us. As David Benner rightly says, 'The life of love is a life of death to the kingdom of self.'[44]

If we are willing to pay the price, it is wonderfully possible for any church to become a community of love and grace within its locality and, as such, to meet the needs of a broken and hurting world. Church growth researcher Christian Schwarz has identified 'loving relationships' as one of the key factors in healthy churches, and says that there is a significant relationship between the ability of a church to demonstrate love and its potential for growth. 'Unfeigned, practical love has a divinely generated magnetic power far more effective than evangelistic programmes which depend almost entirely on verbal communication,' he says. 'People do not want to hear us talk about love, they want to experience how Christian love really works.'[45]

Genuine Christian love is immensely practical. Paul's famous 'hymn to love' in 1 Corinthians 13 describes love not in terms of emotion or sentiment, but in terms of actions and attitudes. 'Love is patient, love is kind. It does not envy, it does not boast, it is not proud. It is not rude, it is not self-seeking, it is not easily angered, it keeps no record of wrongs. Love does not delight in evil but rejoices with the truth. It always protects, always trusts, always hopes, always perseveres' (vv. 4–7). This is the 'most excellent way' (1 Corinthians 12:31) that we are called to follow, which is made possible because of the life of Christ within us. Left to ourselves, it is too high a standard. Only in dependency on Christ, and by abiding in him, can we hope to attain it.

Schwarz talks about a church having its own 'love quotient', a measurable and observable factor in its community life. Certainly, as we read the pages of the New Testament we can begin to see some of the outstanding characteristics of communities of grace. These are the qualities we should desire for every congregation if we are to bear fruit for God and impact a postmodern world with the gospel. What, then, are the identifying marks of a loving community?

A loving community will be a welcoming community. It will open its arms to whomever wishes to come, regardless of their class, ethnic origin, wealth, education, appearance, background and so on. It will be a church without walls or barriers. 'Accept one another, then, just as Christ accepted you,' says Paul (Romans

15:7). His vision for the church was of a place where all divisions between people are taken away. Reconciled to God, we are reconciled to each other: 'There is neither Jew nor Greek, slave nor free, male nor female, for you are all one in Christ Jesus' (Galatians 3:28). Here the lonely find friendship, the outcast acceptance, the fallen forgiveness, the marginalized a home, and the broken healing. The ethos is one of inclusion and welcome, not exclusion and rejection.

A loving community will be a place of acceptance. It will be free of judgmentalism—the insistence that everybody behaves in the same kind of way and shares exactly the same set of beliefs. There is room to breathe, to think, to question, to explore. Certainties are held, but carefully and in love; doubt is not feared and uncertainty is not outlawed. People can grow and develop, knowing that they are loved for who they are and where they are. 'Accept him whose faith is weak,' says Paul, 'without passing judgment on disputable matters' (Romans 14:1). It is a place of safety where the vulnerable can be open, the confused can be heard, the weary can find rest, and the wounded can be restored.

A loving community is a place of appropriate challenge. We only grow if our unacceptable behaviour is confronted lovingly and we are taught more positive ways of behaving. There is a time for encouragement and affirmation, and equally a time for speaking the truth in love (Ephesians 4:15, 25). Transformation occurs when we allow others to get close to us, help us see our blind spots, and then hold us accountable for change. It is a false love that is unwilling to help people put sinful or unhelpful ways behind them. Discipline, too, is an act of grace in community life. Love must sometimes be tough. It is always redemptive in its purpose, however, and seeks the restoration of the person, not their destruction (Galatians 6:1).

A loving community is a place of empowerment. It releases people to develop the full potential of their new life in Christ. It encourages individuals to discover their gifting and to use it for the sake of the body as a whole. 'Each one,' says Peter, 'should use whatever gift he has received to serve others, faithfully administering God's grace in its various forms' (1 Peter 4:10). It is a place of service, both within the community itself and outside in the wider world. The love which is its heartbeat is an outgoing love, and it will find its release in many varied expressions of social action and gospel witness. It will care for the poor and the needy, the sick and the dying, the lost and the helpless. It will reach out to the spiritually hungry, to those of other faiths and none, to the complacent and the self-satisfied. Constrained by the love of Christ, it will proclaim by all possible means the way of salvation.

When church is what Jesus intended it to be, it is the most marvellous place on earth. The outward forms and internal structures may need to change, but at its core it must remain a loving community. There is nothing better than to find ourselves in the midst of a loving, joyful congregation, surrounded by friends who are there to support and encourage us, and share the journey with us. When church maintains its true identity, it can truly be a showcase for God's glory, the best advertisement of all for the gospel. This surely is what Jesus had in mind when he called us to love one another.

✣

The world does not know Jesus
And yet He walks here still.
Ours are the lips that speak His love
We are His hands that heal.

Ours are His feet that tread the earth,
We leave His footprints here.
We breathe His fragrance,
Bear His Name,
We speak:
His voice they hear.

We move with His compassion,
Ache with Him for men's pain,
We cry His tears,
His kindness flows
And makes them whole again.

So let the world see Jesus,
Let His Body move with grace,
That looking at the church He loves,
Men gaze upon His face.

BARBARA PARSONS

QUESTIONS FOR REFLECTION

For individuals

1. Why is answered prayer an outcome of abiding? What are some of the keys to effective prayer? If you were to review your prayer life, what would change?
2. Why is 'joyless Christianity' a contradiction? Why is the kind of joy that Jesus speaks about described as supernatural? How is it different from happiness?
3. How would you define love? What do you think would be the marks of a community based on love? Why do churches so often fail to become communities of grace?
4. Which Christian groups do you belong to? How far do they exhibit the presence of God in terms of (a) answered prayer, (b) supernatural joy and (c) loving community? What can you do to help?
5. What are the shortcomings of solitary religion?

For groups

1. What part does prayer play in the life of your group? What are some of the keys to effective prayer? What change needs to take place within us?
2. Do you think it is right to speak of God as a 'happy' God, and Jesus as a 'man of joy'? Why is joy said to be supernatural? Why are joyful people so attractive to others?
3. How does love express itself practically? What are the four marks of a loving community? Why is love essential for growth?
4. Share from the life of your group or church community examples of (a) answered prayer, (b) times of laughter and joy, and (c) love in action.
5. What part can you as an individual play in making your group more prayerful, more joyful and more loving?

THE CHALLENGE OF THE VINE: LEARNING THE LESSONS

20

IF YOU ABIDE

If you remain in me… (v. 7).

By now it should be obvious that a fruitful life is a real possibility. No matter who we are, it is God's purpose that our lives should bear fruit. If we cooperate with him, he will ensure that it will happen. The life of God within us will inevitably find an outward expression in who we are and what we do.

The little word 'if', however, reminds us that we should not take this for granted. Fruitfulness is not automatic. It requires our active cooperation. We have a choice in the matter. Abiding is the one important condition for fruitfulness, and we have to make a constant choice to abide in Christ on a daily basis. It has to be intentional, not accidental.

Fruitfulness happens when we give ourselves fully to God's purpose. For any true disciple, the aim of their life is to bring glory to God. When we choose to lay aside our own ambitions and goals, and to live instead for the purpose of God, we take the first step towards fruitful living. As we surrender to love and make ourselves available to him without condition or reservation, we are able to respond to his whispered 'Go' in obedience and faith.

Fruitfulness happens as we submit ourselves gladly to his dealings in our lives. There will be times when the Father has to clean us and prune us. We will know his discipline and his training, yet always with the one purpose in mind—that we may bear more fruit. As long as we remember that it is our Father who is at work in our lives, and that all his actions spring from his loving purpose, we will not be dismayed. It will sometimes be painful, and often it will be difficult, but if we understand why he is at work in our lives we can cooperate with him and willingly bring our lives into line with his wise and loving direction for us.

Fruitfulness happens as we build into our lives the 'holy habits' that allow us to draw daily upon his life. This is at the heart of abiding. Spiritual disciplines remind us of our identity in Christ and help us to receive fresh supplies of grace. They are the means by which the life-giving sap flows into the branches, and it is the sap (the very life of Christ) that produces the fruit. As Steve McVey reminds us, 'Fruit on the vine can do nothing to make itself grow. Apart from the vine it has no life. The life of the vine is the life of the branch. Any fruit produced on the branch is the result of the vine flowing through it.'[46]

Fruitfulness happens as we live in conscious dependence upon God. Knowing our weakness and inadequacy, we cry out to God for his help. Choosing not to rely on our own natural strength and ability, we come in our brokenness with the expectation that he will live his life in us and through us. Having learned the *big* lesson that apart from him we can do nothing, we exchange our life for his and happily choose to live in prayerful dependence on the one who works so powerfully within us. It is in our weakness that we are made strong and enabled to bear fruit that lasts.

This is God's design for fruitful living, and it works. As we make abiding in Christ the foundational activity of our lives, we discover that unconsciously and almost without effort, our lives become more productive and satisfying. Not only do we enjoy our own relationship with God more, but we have a greater impact on the world around us. We are blessed ourselves, but also liberated to be a blessing to others. Faith begins to work for us in answered prayer. The life of Jesus fills us with supernatural joy. Love binds us together and moves us to establish communities of grace that can reach out and touch a broken world.

Who knows what God will accomplish through you as you yield your life to him? Who can tell in what exciting and unexpected ways his divine life will express itself through you as you abide in

Christ? Who can imagine where he will lead you or what he will do through you, as you live in dependency upon him?

One thing is certain. If you abide in him, and he abides in you, you will bear much fruit, and so glorify your Father in heaven. Yours will be a fruitful life.

NOTES

1   Rick Warren, *The Purpose Driven Church* (Zondervan, 1995) and *The Purpose Driven Life* (Zondervan, 2002).

2   Andrew Murray, *The True Vine* (Moody Press, 1997 edition), p. 66.

3   The 'I am' sayings of Jesus can be found in John 6:35; 8:12; 10:7; 10:11; 11:25; 14:6; 15:1. The emphasis that is used in the Greek (*ego eimi*) reflects the use of the divine 'I am' in Exodus 3:14, and is clearly intended as a disclosure of Christ's true identity.

4   Matthew Henry's *Commentary* (Marshall Morgan and Scott, 1960), p. 392.

5   Robert Scott Stiner, *Lessons from a Venetian Vinedresser* (Bridge Logos, 2001), and Wayne Jacobsen, *In My Father's Vineyard* (Word Publishing, 1997).

6   Stiner, *Lessons from a Venetian Vinedresser*, p. 122.

7   Jacobsen, *In My Father's Vineyard*, p. 13.

8   Jacobsen, *In My Father's Vineyard*, p. 11.

9   Jacobsen, *In My Father's Vineyard*, p. 16.

10   Jacobsen, *In My Father's Vineyard*, p. 19.

11   Jacobsen, *In My Father's Vineyard*, p. 29.

12   Stiner, *Lessons from a Venetian Vinedresser*, p. 62.

13   Jacobsen, *In My Father's Vineyard*, p. 98.

14   Jacobsen, *In My Father's Vineyard*, p. 105.

15   Selwyn Hughes, *The Divine Gardener* (CWR, 2001)

16   Bruce Wilkinson, *Secrets of the Vine* (Multnomah, 2001), p. 72.

17   Selwyn Hughes, *The Divine Gardener*.

18   James Philip, *Christian Maturity* (IVP, 1964), p. 26.

19   Hudson Taylor, *Union and Communion* (OMF, 1972 edition), p. 5.

20   Richard Foster, *Celebration of Discipline* (Hodder & Stoughton, 1980), p. 6.

21 Dallas Willard, *Spirit of the Disciplines* (Hodder & Stoughton, 1998), p. 160.

22 V. Raymond Edman, *They Found the Secret* (Marshall, Morgan & Scott, 1960), p. 7.

23 Steve McVey, *Grace Walk* (Harvest House Publishers, 1995). See especially the first two chapters.

24 Dr & Mrs Howard Taylor, *Hudson Taylor's Spiritual Secret* (Moody Press, 1989), p. 161.

25 Taylor, *Hudson Taylor's Spiritual Secret*, p. 161.

26 Mike Pilavachi, 'Praying for Revelation', in *Christianity* (March 2004).

27 From the prayer by Ignatius Loyola.

28 Henri Nouwen, *Sabbatical Journey* (DLT, 1998), p. 127.

29ʼ Interviewed on *Songs of Praise*, BBC, October 2004.

30 Witney T. Kuniholm, *Essential 100* (Scripture Union, 2003).

31 Wilkinson, *Secrets of the Vine*, p. 108.

32 Henri Nouwen, *The Return of the Prodigal* (DLT, 1994), p. 39.

33 Brennan Manning, *Abba's Child* (NavPress, 1994), p. 50.

34 David Benner, *Sacred Companions* (IVP, 2002), pp. 30–31 and *Surrender to Love* (IVP, 2003), p. 28.

35 Norman Grubb, *Rees Howells: Intercessor* (Lutterworth Press, 1972).

36 Benner, *Surrender to Love*, p. 58.

37 Benner, *Surrender to Love*, p. 66.

38 Andrew Murray, *Abide in Christ* (Barbour, 1985), p. 138.

39 John Dalrymple, *Simple Prayer* (DLT, 1984), p. 17.

40 Dalrymple, *Simple Prayer*, pp. 114–115.

41 See, for example, Richard Buckner, *The Joy of Jesus* (Canterbury Press, 1993) and Wanda Nash, *Come Let Us Play* (DLT, 1999).

42 Sheila Walsh, *Honestly* (Hodder & Stoughton, 1996), pp. 165, 186–187.

43 Benner, *Surrender to Love*, p. 90.

44 Benner, *Surrender to Love*, p. 91.

45 Christian Schwarz, *Natural Church Development* (BCGA, 1996), p. 36.
46 Steve McVey, *Grace Walk* (Harvest House Publishers, 1995), p. 170.

SONG OF THE SHEPHERD

Meeting the God of grace in Psalm 23

Of all the psalms written by King David, the most popular and well-known is Psalm 23, yet its very familiarity may lead us to miss its beauty and fail to hear its message. This book shows that the picture of the loving shepherd and his sheep speaks profoundly about how we can relate to God. It invites us to enjoy a relationship of intimacy and grace, finding true peace and contentment as we learn to depend on him day by day.

Song of the Shepherd examines the psalm verse by verse and can be used either for individual reflection or for group discussion (questions provided). It covers key issues in discipleship for both new and mature Christians—learning how to rest in God, learning to trust him through the difficult times, and learning how to live from the resources he provides.

ISBN 1 84101 291 2   £6.99
Available from your local Christian bookshop or, in case of difficulty, direct from BRF using the order form on page 160.

WITH JESUS IN THE UPPER ROOM

Forty Gospel reflections from John 13–17

DAVID WINTER

This book invites us to spend forty days reflecting on five key chapters of John's Gospel, the so-called 'Upper Room Discourses' which record the conversation between Jesus and his disciples on the night before he died. As we read, we can imagine ourselves sitting with those disciples as the darkness falls outside while the light among them grows brighter and brighter. Through the ears, eyes and memory of the 'Beloved Disciple' who recalled what took place long after the event, we can share in the wonder of a quite extraordinary evening.

ISBN 1 84101 324 2   £6.99
Available from your local Christian bookshop or, in case of difficulty, direct from BRF using the order form on page 160.

ALONG THE DISCIPLESHIP ROAD

Following Jesus today

JAY COLWILL

By choosing to follow Jesus, setting off on the road of discipleship, we embark upon an adventure that will challenge us and take us into unknown territory. Along the way we will surely face all kinds of 'hills', times of struggle that present us with a stark challenge: do we press on, growing in strength and determination, or do we give up and turn back?

This book explores what we can learn from the stories of some of Jesus' disciples: Andrew, Peter, James, Mary Magdalene, Thomas and Matthew. Their experiences, their triumphs and failures of faith and, above all, their relationship with Jesus offer us help and guidance as we seek to follow him as disciples today.

ISBN 1 84101 401 X   £6.99
Available from your local Christian bookshop or, in case of difficulty, direct from BRF using the order form on page 160.

ON THIS ROCK

Bible foundations for Christian living

STEPHEN COTTRELL

'As you read this book I hope you will learn to love the Bible, and be excited by its claims and challenges. But, more importantly, I hope you will be led closer to Jesus.'

Stephen Cottrell has written this book for new Christians who want to grow in their faith and for more experienced Christians who want to re-set the compass of their discipleship. In 28 Bible readings telling the story of the apostle Peter, he explores what being a disciple meant back then, and how it relates to the life of a disciple today. As well as teaching about how to grow as a follower of Jesus, the book will help establish a regular pattern for Bible reading, reflection and prayer.

ISBN 1 84101 238 6   £3.99
Available from your local Christian bookshop or, in case of difficulty, direct from BRF using the order form on page 160.

TRANSFORMING THE ORDINARY

Bible meditations for the everyday

JOHN HENSTRIDGE

Like John Henstridge's first book, *Step into the Light* (BRF, 2000), this book is a series of prayer meditations based around Bible passages. The focus of *Transforming the Ordinary* is on helping us build awareness of God into the variety and ordinariness of our daily routines.

From celebrating a birthday to being stuck in a queue of traffic, the thirty meditations cover a range of familiar experiences and events, showing how we can learn, whatever our circumstances, to tune our hearts and minds into God's presence, there with us. The meditations can be used by individuals for their own personal prayer time, but the introduction also suggests ways of making use of them in a group setting.

ISBN 1 84101 316 1   £6.99
Available from your local Christian bookshop or, in case of difficulty, direct from BRF using the order form on page 160.

You may be interested to know that Tony Horsfall is a regular contributor to *New Daylight*, BRF's popular series of Bible reading notes. *New Daylight* is ideal for those looking for a devotional approach to reading and understanding the Bible. Each issue covers four months of daily Bible reading and reflection, a Bible passage (text included), helpful comment and a prayer or thought for the day ahead.

New Daylight is written by a gifted team of contributors including Adrian Plass, David Winter, Gordon Giles, Rachel Boulding, Peter Graves, Helen Julian CSF, David Spriggs, Margaret Silf, Jenny Robertson and Veronica Zundel.

NEW DAYLIGHT SUBSCRIPTIONS

❏ I would like to give a gift subscription
(please complete both name and address sections below)
❏ I would like to take out a subscription myself
(complete name and address details only once)

This completed coupon should be sent with appropriate payment to BRF. Alternatively, please write to us quoting your name, address, the subscription you would like for either yourself or a friend (with their name and address), the start date and credit card number, expiry date and signature if paying by credit card.

Gift subscription name _____

Gift subscription address _____

_____ Postcode _____

Please send to the above, beginning with the next January/May/September issue: (delete as applicable)

(please tick box)	UK	SURFACE	AIR MAIL
NEW DAYLIGHT	❏ £12.00	❏ £13.35	❏ £15.60
NEW DAYLIGHT 3-year sub	❏ £29.55		

Please complete the payment details below and send your coupon, with appropriate payment to: **BRF, First Floor, Elsfield Hall, 15–17 Elsfield Way, Oxford OX2 8FG**

Your name _____

Your address _____

_____ Postcode _____

Total enclosed £ _____ (cheques should be made payable to 'BRF')

Payment by cheque ❏ postal order ❏ Visa ❏ Mastercard ❏ Switch ❏

Card number: ☐☐☐☐☐☐☐☐☐☐☐☐☐☐☐☐☐☐☐

Expiry date of card: ☐☐☐☐ Issue number (Switch): ☐☐☐☐

Signature (essential if paying by credit/Switch card) _____

❏ Please do not send me further information about BRF publicaations.

NB: BRF notes are also available from your local Christian bookshop. **BRF is a Registered Charity**

ORDER FORM

REF	TITLE	PRICE	QTY	TOTAL
291 2	*Song of the Shepherd*	£6.99		
324 2	*With Jesus in the Upper Room*	£6.99		
401 X	*Along the Discipleship Road*	£6.99		
238 6	*On This Rock*	£3.99		
316 1	*Transforming the Ordinary*	£6.99		

POSTAGE AND PACKING CHARGES

order value	UK	Europe	Surface	Air Mail
£7.00 & under	£1.25	£3.00	£3.50	£5.50
£7.01–£30.00	£2.25	£5.50	£6.50	£10.00
Over £30.00	free	prices on request		

Postage and packing:

Donation:

Total enclosed:

Name _____ Account Number _____

Address_____

_____ Postcode _____

Telephone Number _____ Email _____

Payment by: ☐ Cheque ☐ Mastercard ☐ Visa ☐ Postal Order ☐ Switch

Card no. ☐☐☐☐ ☐☐☐☐ ☐☐☐☐ ☐☐☐☐

Expires ☐☐ ☐☐   Issue no. of Switch card ☐☐☐

Signature _____ Date _____

All orders must be accompanied by the appropriate payment.

Please send your completed order form to:
BRF, First Floor, Elsfield Hall, 15–17 Elsfield Way, Oxford OX2 8FG
Tel. 01865 319700 / Fax. 01865 319701 Email: enquiries@brf.org.uk

☐ Please send me further information about BRF publications.

Available from your local Christian bookshop.   BRF is a Registered Charity